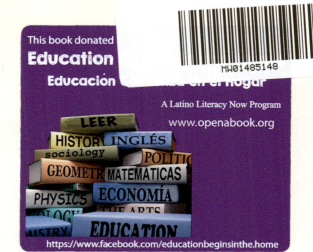

UNIVERSAL MIND:

New Way to
Mystic Power
and Prosperity

UNIVERSAL MIND:

New Way to
Mystic Power
and Prosperity

Robert A. Ferguson

PARKER PUBLISHING COMPANY, INC.

West Nyack, NY

© 1979 *by*

Parker Publishing Company, Inc.
West Nyack, N.Y.

Library of Congress Cataloging in Publication Data

Ferguson, Robert A
    Universal Mind.

    1. Success. 2. Occult sciences. I. Title.
BJ1611.2.F463   131'.32   78-13624
ISBN 0-13-938035-3

Printed in the United States of America

Also by the Author

Psychic Telemetry: New Key to Health, Wealth and Perfect Living

To David Nelson Early

WHAT THIS BOOK CAN DO FOR YOU

There are a few "lucky" people who are successful, healthy, and happy. They seem to accomplish anything they set out to do. They have an endless source of energy and that extra amount of good luck.

If you are not one of these lucky people and instead find yourself short of money, find that your love-life is a disappointment, feel as if you're stuck in a rut or are just generally frustrated with life, then you need this book. This book was written for you and people just like you who are attempting to overcome the perplexities of life.

SUCCESS, HEALTH, AND HAPPINESS ARE MORE THAN GOOD LUCK

This book will lift you from poverty to prosperity, from loneliness to love, from pessimism to optimistic happiness—to increased health and vigor, a new youthfulness. All of these things, and even more are yours—right now, just for the asking.

YOU NEVER AGAIN NEED FACE DEFEAT

Have people used you and abused you while they claw their way to success? Do you feel intimidated by the power or wealth of others? You shouldn't!

This book will teach you how to "zap" those people right out of your life. You'll reward your friends and punish your enemies. You need never again suffer the feelings of defeat. You will control a power so awesome that you never again need feel fear toward any living creature. You will unquestionably be the *master* of your own world. Long before you finish the first chapter of this book, you will discover that success, happiness, love, and health are more than good luck.

HOW MARILEE M. GAINED A PROMOTION

Marilee M. had been passed over again and again for promotion even though she out-performed her fellow workers. One zap from Marilee and a ton of cement dropped from a freeway overpass onto the hood of her boss' car. She got her promotion.

AL BECAME A FIRST TIME FATHER
AT FIFTY-TWO

"You'll never have children," the doctor told Al. Twenty-five years later, Al became a father at fifty-two and then again at fifty-seven.

JUAN S. USED UNIVERSAL MIND POWER
TO BECOME A SUCCESSFUL CHICKEN RANCHER

Juan S. had no money when he reached the United States from the Phillipines. Like many immigrants before him, he believed achieving riches would be a very simple thing.

Juan floundered in poverty until his American sponsor took him to a Cosmonomics class.

Today, Juan is happily married, and a very wealthy chicken rancher who spends many months each year at his beautiful vacation home in Guatemala.

YOU TOO CAN BECOME A MIRACLE WORKER

I don't claim to be a scholar, but I do claim that I've discovered how to use the miraculous cosmic energy that surrounds me—and surrounds *you*. And I'm going to prove that you have this same miraculous power at your own fingertips. Are you ready to perform a universal mind miracle? If you are, keeping reading further into this book. The Great Cosmic Mind wants you to be rich in mind and body, and you can be! Long before you finish reading this book, you will be performing miracle after miracle, and miracles again. The proven practices and techniques in this book put you in instant touch with the great Universal Mind or Cosmos, which means precisely the same thing. Many of the methods are therefore called Cosmonomic, indicating the propelling laser-like energy within the Universal Mind.

PETER H. DOUBLED HIS SALARY FOR FOUR CONSECUTIVE YEARS

Peter H. was the average middle-aged suburbanite. He had a middle class home, a wife and children. His life was steady but uneventful. He doubted that his life would ever change a great deal.

"Once you reach middle-age, your chances for promotions and more money are pretty slim," he said.

But Peter discovered Universal Mind Power and doubled his salary in each of four consecutive years. A miracle? Not really, just the proper application of Cosmonomic principles.

THE POWER OF UNIVERSAL ULTRA MIND IS NOT AN INDIVIDUALIZED POWER SOURCE

Universal Mind Power is life itself. It is the psychic energy that flows through, and out of, every created object within the world.

Universal Cosmonomic power is a combination of the latest in scientific discovery, ancient mysticism, occultism, religious writings, folklore, and good old common sense. Universal Ultra-Mind Power draws energy from all of these sources and combines the best ingredients of each to produce miracles—miracles of incredible attainment.

BETTY F. THREW AWAY HER
CRUTCHES AND WALKED

Betty F. was making plans to leave her job and apply for disability insurance. After a few treatments with Meta-Cosmonomic Finger Pressure she threw away her crutches and walked unaided, and without pain.

I'M GOING TO TEACH YOU WHAT
I *KNOW* WORKS

When I tell you that I'm going to change your life, I mean it! I am not giving you false hopes. I'm only going to tell you what I *know* works. I don't have to make idle promises of rich rewards when I've seen Universal Mind miracles happen time after time.

I can honestly tell you that there is not one material possession that I have ever wanted that I do not have. Many people have nick-named me "Happy." And why not? I am happy and I am prosperous—and I didn't fulfill all of my desires by hard work. It's true that I just didn't sit around and let things fall into my lap. I studied Universal Mind Power and let it do the work for me.

Simply speaking, I pushed the Universal Mind Power button and all of life-energy went to work to fulfill my every need.

I accomplished my dreams, and you are going to accomplish yours—not in months or years, but in seconds, hours, or days.

What do you want? Fame? Power? Money? Health? Love? Happiness? You don't have to make the choice—every one of these things can be yours for the asking. And this book is going to show you how to accomplish what I accomplished, and even more.

YOU HOLD THE KEY TO A UNIVERSAL MIND MIRACLE

Everyone believes that there must be a secret key to open the floodgates of the psychic miracles. Let me assure you before you read any further, *there is such a secret key.* And that key is your desire for a more happy, healthful, and productive life. Your desire, plus the occult secrets that are taught in this book, create miracle after miracle.

The mechanics of working a miracle are very simple if you have someone to guide you along the way. And that is exactly what I am going to do! I will give you the step-by-step instruction you need to turn your dreams into positive realities.

SHIRLEY F. WANTED A KNIGHT
IN SHINING ARMOR

Lonely Shirley F. had resigned herself to a life of spinsterhood. She studied the principles of Universal Mind Power and was happily married within weeks.

"I didn't get a knight in shining armor," she wrote, "but he literally did come riding into my life upon a white horse. I just can't believe how happy I really am."

THERE IS A SUBCONSCIOUS COSMIC CODE

From the depths of eternity pulsates a cosmic code. A cosmic code that any person can quickly learn to decipher. The Cosmonomic code penetrates your subconscious mind 24-hours of every day. Through the use of dominos and ordinary playing cards, I will teach you to read these Cosmonomic codes. I will teach you to forecast the future or to test your own Cosmonomic powers with what many people look upon as simple games of entertainment.

MELANEE O. SPENT 10¢ TO WIN $500

Melanee O. had never gambled in her entire life, but while on a vacation trip through California, Melanee and her family stopped at South Lake Tahoe for lunch. On the spur of the moment, Melanee dropped two nickles into a slot machine. She won a $500 jackpot.

UNIVERSAL MIND POWER REQUIRES
LITTLE EFFORT ON YOUR PART

Other than having the desire to perform a miracle, as I've previously mentioned, Cosmonomics take little time from your busy day. Cosmonomic Power does not rely upon deep study and concentration. It relies upon the miracle ingredients that are right now at your very fingertips.

I become so enthusiastic over the happiness, wealth, and health that have come to my students. I find it difficult to cut off my words. But this is only the introduction to *Universal Mind*.

Turn to Chapter One and begin reading. It won't be long before you'll be saying "I believe in miracles."

Robert A. Ferguson

Contents

What This Book Can Do for You . 7

1. **How To Tune In, and Turn On, Your Miraculous Powers of Universal Mind . 23**

   How to Use Universal Mind Power. How to Avoid the Common Mystical Pitfall. How to Tune Your Consciousness Toward the Ultra-Mind Power. You Are Now In Attunement with the Ultra-Cosmonomic Mind. Learn to Express Your Desires. Begin a Notebook of Desires. How to Unleash Your Ultra-Cosmonomic Power. The Fulfillment of Your Own Desires Will Never Harm Another Person. How to Strengthen Your Universal Cosminomic Power. Develop the Art of Observation. The Ritual That Will Build Your Seven Cosmonomic Energy Centers. How to Begin Your Magic Ritual. How to Recharge Your Cosmonomic Batteries. Make Sure That You Really Want What You're Asking For. How Sharon L. Used Cosmonomics to Win the Man She Loved. Common Sense Will Improve Your Cosmonomic Power Performance. Cosmonomic Characteristics That Should Be Incorporated Into Your Daily Life. Don't Waste Your New Found Powers Trying to

13

1. **How To Tune In, and Turn On, Your Miraculous Powers of Universal Mind (cont.)**

Convince the Skeptic . You Can Change Anything In Your Life If Your Timing Is Right . How Nelson E. Borrowed $3,000 and Turned It Into $40,000 Within Six Months .

2. **How Dominos Bring You Love and Prosperity Through a Mystic Universal Mind Code . 45**

A Set of Dominos Can Answer Your Every Question . The Ancient Chinese Were the First to Use Dominos . The Coded Dots Speak to Every Man . How Dominos Point to Future Events . Dominos Foretell, They Do Not Compel . How to Acquire Your Dominos . The Ritual That Will Attune You to the Secret Cosmic Code . How to Care For Your Dominos . How the Divining Dominos Led George M. to a Rich and Successful Life . How to Use Your Dominos to Foretell the Future . Pronounce the Magic Word as You Stir the Dominos . The One Domino Draw . The Diviner May Not Draw a Donimo to Forecast His Own Future . How to Read the Code of the One Domino Draw . How to Read the Cosmic Code (The Eastern Method). How to Use the Western Method to Read the Cosmonomic Code . The Unlucky Dominos . Domino Doubles ·Hold a Special Meaning . General Domino Interpretations . How to Read the Cosmic Codes . The Future of Two People Can Be Forecast at One Sitting . Both Persons Must Stir the Dominos . How to Forecast the Future for a Full Year . The Astrological Twelve Domino Draw . How to Interpret the Astrological Forecast . Weave the Cosmic Code Into a Story . The Twelve Domino Astrological Cosmic Code . If You Don't Like the Future, Change It! .

3. **Universal Medi-Cosmonomic Finger Pressure Can Bring You Perfect Health . 65**

Cosmic Finger Pressure Can Either Cure or Prevent an Illness . Cosmic Finger Pressure has been Practiced Since the Dawn of Humanity . Medi-Cosmonomic Finger Pressure Is not Medicine . Cosmonomic Finger Pressure Is Simple . Finger

3. **Universal Medi-Cosmonomic Finger Pressure Can Bring You Perfect Health (cont.)**

Pressure Therapy Is Pleasant . How Cosmonomics Prevents and Cures an Illness . How You Can Become a Cosmonomic Finger Pressure Therapist . The Powerful Ritual That Will Fill Your Fingers With Cosmic Energy . How to Test Your New Found Cosmic Power . Cosmic Finger Pressure Left Robert F. Pain Free . The Curious Case of Betty B.'s Arthritis . The Seven Wonders of Cosmonomic Finger Prssure . How to Use Cosmic Finger Pressure Therapy Effectively . How to Begin Your Cosmic Therapy . How to Perform the Cosmic Finger Pressure Therapy . Perform Your Cosmic Therapy Weekly . The Body's Energy Centers Are Numerous But Easily Located . Cosmic Finger Pressure Therapy (Top of the Head Area) . The Back of the Neck Therapy . How to Perform Finger Pressure Therapy in the Facial Area . Each Pressure Point is to be Pressed Three Times . Side-of-the-Neck Finger Pressure is Valuable Therapy . How to Correct Problems of the Foot, Ankle, and Toe . How to Use Cosmic Therapy Pressure Upon the Fingers and the Palm . Finger Pressure Upon the Sides of the Heel . Prevent Pains in the Heart, Paralysis, Cramps, Gout, Strained Muscles, and Writer's Cramp with Forearm Cosmic Therapy . Finger Pressure Therapy and the Abdomen . Cosmic Finger Pressure and the Leg . Let the Miracle of Medi-Cosmonomic Power Bring you Success, Money, Happiness, Love, Power, and Perfect Health, Forever .

4. **Herbs, Spices and Folklore: Nature's Amazing Universal Mind Medicine . 91**

You Already Are A Psychic Healer . One Man's Weed Is Another Man's Herb . How Gordon L. and Vern B. Restored Hair to Their Balding Heads . The Catalyst That Makes the Herb a Magic Medicine . How Herbs Can Protect the Lungs of Cigarette Smokers . "Wonder Drugs" are Usually Culled From Ancient Folklore . How You Can Become a Cosmonomic Medicine Man . The Powerful Initiation Ritual Into the Society of Cosmonomic Medicine Men . What Is an Herb? . When

4.   Herbs, Spices and Folklore: Nature's Amazing Universal Mind Medicine (cont.)

Modern Antibiotics Failed, The Doctor Turned To Papaya Fruit . Don't Ignore the Medical Profession . Dennis P.'s Rheumatism was Diagnosed as Incurable. A Change of Diet Left Him Pain Free. . Most Medicines Purchased From the Drugstore Can Be Found in the Average Home . How Medi-Cosmonomic Medicine Cured Mable T.'s Hypertension . How to Give Your Herbs Even More Magic Power . When to Gather Your Herbs . Additional Tips for Herb Gathering and Storage . Science Announces "New" Poison Antidote . Helen M.'s Psoriasis was Thought Incurable Until She Discovered Sarsaparilla . Medi-Cosmonomic Medicine Works Best When Your Body is on an "Up" Cycle . How to Discover the High and Low Days of Your Physical Cycle . How to Prevent or Slow Down Hardening of the Arteries . How Leona M. Threw Away Her Diet and Lost Forty Pounds . Don't Overlook the Importance of Your "Declaration" as You Make Your Herbs Ready for Use . How to Use Nature's Universal Cosmonomic Medicine . How Ron R. Cured His Migraine Headaches by Eating Cabbage . How Vernal A. Used Lemon Peel to Clear His Skin and Look Ten Years Younger . Here's to Your New and Longer Life of Greater Health and Vitality.

5.   Dynamic Universal Mind Rituals, Chants, and Affirmations to Bring You All the Money, Love, and Success You Can Use . 115

Chants and Rituals are Mystic Cosmic Vibrations . Money Has Always been a Troublemaker . What is Money? . Your First Step Upon the Path to Cosmonomic Prosperity . Cosmonomic Prosperity's Second Step . The Cosmonomic Prosperity Current . Prosperity! Step Four . How You Can Quickly Lose All of Your Financial Gains . When Arthur F. Agreed to Unselfishly Give Away Money He Could Not Afford, a Cosmonomic Miracle Occurred . Adjust Short Term Appearances for Long Term Goals . Let Money Do More Than Buy Material Possessions . The Powerful Prosperity Ritual That Gives You the King Midas Golden Touch . How Marvin L.

5. **Dynamic Universal Mind Rituals, Chants, and Affirmations to Bring You All the Money, Love, and Success You Can Use (cont.)**

Went From Common Laborer to Construction Foreman . The Mystic Chant That Will Win Contests . How Marianne K. Won a New Automobile Two Years in a Row at the Church Bazaar . A Second Powerful Affirmation That Brings You Money and Success . How This Author Used Affirmations to Write Psychic Telemetry . The Cosmonomic Ritual That Brings Success Every Time . How to Perform the Cosmonomic Success Ritual . How to End Your Mystic Ritual . Program Your Subconscious Mind to Work for You 24 Hours a Day . How to Program Your Subconscious Mind to Work for Your While You Peacefully Sleep Away the Hours . How Ethyl B. Used a Chant to Frighten Her Attacker Away . The Mystic Chant Works Only Against Evil . The Mystic Chant for Self-Protection . How to Win Friends and Influence People . The Secret Chant That Will Win All of the Friendships you Can Possibly Desire . The Affirmation That Will Influence the Thoughts of Others . The Psychic Declaration That Affirms Your Perfect Health . Keep Your Perspective: All Areas of Your Life are Interrelated.

6. **Power Your Way to Love, Happiness, and Protection From Evil With Universal Mind Magic . 137**

The Ancient Mystics Learned That The "Cosmos Thought Force" Was a Powerful and Very Welcome Occult Tool . You Have Probably Already Been the Victim of an Evil Cosmos Thought Force . How Donald G. Broke Through the Cosmos Thought Force of an Evil, Vindictive Woman . How to Protect Yourself From an Evil Cosmos Thought Force . How to Build Your Protective Wall of Psychic Energy . How to Dispose of the Psychic Sand Used in Your Ritual . What Is a Cosmos Thought Force? . How You Can Use Your Own Powerful Cosmos Thought Force to Bend Others to Your Will . Remember These Important Psychic Rules . How Karen X. Used Her Powerful

6.   Power Your Way to Love, Happiness, and Protection From Evil With Universal Mind Magic (cont.)

Cosmic Thought Force to Land a Role on Broadway . How Eugene Z. Used His Powerful Universal Mind Thought Force to Regain the Inheritance That He Had Been Cheated Out Of . How Color Can Bring Love, Health and Happiness Into Your Life . Helen G. Used Her Cosmonomic Color Code and Was Married In One Week . How to Use Your Own Cosmonomic Color Table . General Color Interpretations . The Colors That Others Wear Are Secret Cosmonomic Signs That Can Be Read By You . Color Can Make Any Wish A Reality . How Andrea S. Used Her Cosmonomic Color Knowledge to Quadruple Her Business In Just One Year . Don't Let the Powerful Use of Color Backfire on You . How Elaine E. Suffered the Consequences When She Forgot to Use Her Common Sense . Health, Wealth, Success, and Happiness Is More Than Luck . How To Determine You Own Lucky Numbers . How To Use Your Numbers . The Magical Ritual That Gives Your Lucky Numbers Greater Cosmonomic Power . How Marlene D. Used Her Nine Lucky Numbers to Win Over $10,000 . How to Use Your Lucky Numbers . How You Can Forecast Your Lucky Day .

7.   Put Your Miraculous Universal Mind Power Into Action With a Deck of Ordinary Playing Cards . 159

A Deck of Playing Cards Gives All the Answers . Ancient Egyptian Adepts Hid Their Secret Knowledge in Playing Cards . Cards Speak in Universal Cosmonomic Code . How the Cards Point to Miraculous Signs . The Cards Foretell, They Do Not Compel . How to Acquire Your Decks of Cards . How to Make Your Cards a Magic Deck . The Unity of Man Deck . The Powerful Ritual That Will Make The Cards Speak to You . How to Care for Your Cards . How Eden G. Discovered That a Man Loved Her . How to Use Your Unity of Man Deck . How to Interpret the Cards . Reading the Physical and Psychological States of Being . How to Interpret the Spiritual State of Being . Your Wheel of Fortune Cards Will Answer Every Question .

7. Put Your Miraculous Universal Mind Power Into Action With a Deck of Ordinary Playing Cards (cont.)

What the Suits of Cards in Your Deck Represent . How to Use Your Wheel of Fortune Cards . How to Read the Wheel of Fortune Cards . How Jerry H. Failed to Heed the Cards and Lost Everything He Owned . How to Interpret Your Wheel of Fortune Cards . Let Your Cards Be the Sign of a New and Prosperous Life.

8. Perfecting Your Universal Mind Power to Open New Doors of Expression, Fulfullment, and Accomplishment. 185

Know Who You Are! . How to Play the Game of Life . How to "Zap" the Person Who Places a Roadblock in Your Path of Life . How Merilee M. Zapped Her Boss and Won a Promotion . Use a Three Step Approach to Reach Your Ultra-Cosmonomic Power Level . How to Earn the Special Attention of the Creative Universal Mind . How to Preprare Yourself to Receive a Miracle . Attune Yourself to Mystic Forces . You Cannot Avoid Conflict . Be Prepared to Fight For What Is Yours . What You Do With Your Miracle Depends Upon You . Retain Balance If You Wish to Succeed . You're Never Too Old to Experience the Fullness of Life . Alvin C. Became a Father at Fifty-Two . Become a Psychic Athlete . Advanced Universal Mind Secrets . The Mystic Chart to Win Friends and Influence People . How a County Planning Commission Reversed Its Action After Fred H. Performed His Mystic Chant . How to Perform the Mystic Chant That Will Influence Others . How to Chant Love Into Your Life . The Chant of the North . How Elaine F. Became Belle of the Ball . Love Chant of the South . Love Chant of the West . How Norman N. Used the Love Chant of the West to Win the Perfect Mate . Love Chant of the East . The General Purpose Chant . Though the Origin of Lucky Charms Is Lost In Antiquity Their Power Remains . Why Your Lucky Charm or Talisman Generates Power . Lucinda V. Made Her Own Lucky Charm and Won the Man She Loved . The Universal Ritual That Will Create a Lucky Charm . How

8. Perfecting Your Universal Mind Power to Open New Doors of Expression, Fulfullment, and Accomplishment (cont.)

to Use Gems to Bring Love, Happiness, and Prosperity Into Your Life . The Blue Gems Are Your Spiritual Gems . How Alfred L. Used a Powerful Gem to Break a Life-Long Curse . The Red Gems are Your Physical Stones . How to Gain Emotional Security by Wearing Green Stones . Yellow Gems Govern the Intellect . The Diamond Will Attract Prosperity . The Gemstone Power Affirmation . There Can Be No Excuse for Clinging to an Unhappy Life . Let Your New Universal Mind Power Bring Ecstasy, Plentitude, and Abundant Health .

UNIVERSAL MIND:

New Way to
Mystic Power
and Prosperity

Chapter One

HOW TO TUNE IN, AND TURN ON, YOUR MIRACULOUS POWERS OF UNIVERSAL MIND

If Universal Mind were just a party game or a frivolous gesture of a new form of entertainment, there would be no reason for me to write this book or for you to read it. *Universal Mind* is a serious adventure with very practical applications. Are you lonely? You needn't be. Universal Mind will teach you how to acquire your desired companionship. Unlucky? It can bring good luck beyond your wildest dreams. Money? That needn't be a problem any longer. Universal Mind establishes a special relationship between yourself and the great Cosmic Mind that rules the universe. Never again will you be left out of the good things in

life. You're beginning the most exciting adventure of your life—
attunement with the Infinite Power of Good.

HOW TO USE UNIVERSAL MIND POWER

The Universal Mind approach to fulfillment is one of action.
A minimum of your efforts are required for meditation or unneeded mental gymnastics. Cosmonomics reasons that the great
unseen forces which created the universe must still be operating,
or the universe would collapse back into a nothingness. Directing
these miraculous forces of Cosmonomic power influences the
course of creation and makes you truly a miracle worker. The cor-
nerstone of Cosmonomics is achievement—Not wishful thinking
or a false hope, but a positive demonstration that any wish can
become a reality.

HOW TO AVOID THE COMMON MYSTICAL PITFALL

The most common of the mystical pitfalls is the development
of a beautiful and loving impracticability toward existence.

Universal Mind can be coldly calculating, for its demonstration rests upon strict adherence to set laws and principles. Resting
solely upon the demonstration of cosmonomic miracles without
regard to human feelings can result in unflattering cases of exces-
sive egotism. Excesses in either direction can slow, and gradually
bring to a halt, all of the gains that you have acquired through the
use of the creative forces that are at work around you at this very
moment.

The most wholesome approach to Universal Mind Power is
one of balance. Combine the practical Law of Universal Mind
with the warmth of mystical experience so that self-improvement
is manifested in every facet of your life. The richer and fuller your
life, the more you are fulfilling your destiny as a healthy, happy,
and prosperous individual.

HOW TO TUNE YOUR CONSCIOUSNESS TOWARD
THE ULTRA-MIND POWER

You've already taken and conquered the most difficult first
step toward Cosmonomic realization.

By reading these first few pages of the book you have expressed not only the desire to improve your life, but the willingness to put a little effort toward the manifestation of cosmonomic miracles.

The remainder of the "attunement process" is quite easy. You must only recognize what a powerful person you really are. And how do you do this? Simple!

1. *You are one of the most powerful creative forces in the universe.*

   When man first appeared upon the earth he was endowed with all of the creative forces of Nature. Only through neglect of this power can man be unhappy, ill, or burdened by poverty.

2. *Accept the fact that you can perform miracles.*

   Don't waste your time trying to understand how and why Cosmonomics can perform miracles. First achieve your every dream. Only after you bask in the glory of your dreams fulfilled should you spend the time to intellectually consider the "why" and "how" of Ultra-Cosmonomic Power. Get what you want first—erase all of the problems from your life. When you've done this, you'll have plenty of time to philosophize upon the miracle of Universal Mind dynamics.

3. *Know that cosmonomic energy is ready to flow through you 24 hours a day.*

   Cosmonomic energy, or its creative force, is not waiting in a vast emptiness of space for you to seek it out and find it. Miracle power surrounds you every minute of your life. It is in you and around you. You are never without it. You cannot exist without it.

It's true you cannot exist without cosmonomic power. You'll notice I said you "cannot exist without it." I didn't say you had to use the power. Conscious acceptance of cosmonomic power leads to health, wealth, and happiness. Refusal to recognize and use the power leads to poverty and despair. But even when surrounded by the negative influences of a materialistic world, the power is there. You only have to want to use it.

YOU ARE NOW IN ATTUNEMENT WITH
THE ULTRA-COSMONOMIC MIND

Did you hear bells ringing? Feel faint, or suddenly uplifted? You shouldn't have!

In the paragraphs above, I was subtly addressing my words to your subconscious mind—telling it to wake up and go to work. And as your subconscious mind awakened to my prodding you should have little, if any new sensations. I didn't bestow a new and unfamiliar power upon you; I quite simply put into action a power that has always been a vital part of your existence—you just haven't used it in the most constructive manner. But you will from this moment on! You're about to perform your very first miracle.

LEARN TO EXPRESS YOUR DESIRES

Surprisingly, many people are unhappy and they really don't know what it would take to make them happy. And then again, there is the small circle of persons who actually enjoy being miserable. Obviously the miraculous cosmonomic power is going to do absolutely nothing for them. Don't waste your time trying to understand why these people act as they do while willingly enduring the misery under which they live. Spend your time in a useful and constructive manner—first upon solving your own problems, and then when that has been accomplished help others along the way. But until you have everything you want, you are really in no position to worry unduly about those who have the same opportunities available to them, but refuse to use them.

Don't let yourself fall into this trap of acceptance of negative conditions in your own life. It takes no effort whatsoever to be miserable and little effort to be happy and prosperous. Select the best of the two choices—ultimate richness and happiness. But before you can expect the miracles to tumble around you, you must first learn to express your desires.

A simple statement such as, "I want to be happy," is not sufficient to put your Cosmonomic forces to work. You must be explicit. You must know what it is you want that will make you happy.

Do you want money? How much money do you want? What do you want it for?

Do you want better health? Why?

Do you want to win a contest? If you do win, what good will it do you?

Know what you want and be able to express what you want.

BEGIN A NOTEBOOK OF DESIRES

If you can't perform a cosmonomic miracle it's because you haven't really understood what you're asking for or why you want it.

The easiest way to make positive expressions of your wants and needs is to keep a small notebook in which you write your secret desires. This is the time to be specific, and your notebook is a handy reminder that your miracles are happening as you check them from the pages, one by one. I call my own notebook, *My Wants and Why Book.*

Step One: Write down exactly what you want.

Step Two: Write down exactly why you want it.

Step Three: Let the creative force of your cosmonomic power go to work.

HOW TO UNLEASH YOUR ULTRA-COSMONOMIC POWER

Your conscious mind is very much like a modern computer. It can handle and solve the most complex of problems, but the computer must be programmed accurately with all data possible before it can produce accurate solutions to problems. The computer cannot make decisions or judgments upon things it was not programmed to do.

The frustration you feel when confronted with a seemingly unsolvable problem is natural. You're frustrated because you are using the wrong mental computer.

Only the power of your subconscious mind sets you apart from the brilliant computer. Your subconscious mind furnishes you with the necessary missing data so that your cosmonomic power can go to work for you.

When you have decided what you want and why you want it, you can turn your problem loose with your subconscious mind by a simple statement:

> I now express my desire to my subconscious mind. (Say what it is that you want).
>
> The creative force of my Ultra-Cosmonomic Power is set free to perform my miracle, and to bring it quickly to me.

THE FULFILLMENT OF YOUR OWN DESIRES
WILL NEVER HARM ANOTHER PERSON

At this step upon the path to the ultimate satisfaction of experiencing cosmonomic miracles, you might have some self-doubts, or you might even wonder if you are doing the right thing. Let me assure you that you *are* doing the right thing. Man was meant to have the best of everything and that's exactly what is going to happen to you.

Any doubt that you may be experiencing is probably caused by a mistaken belief that your gain must be someone else's loss. Cosmonomics doesn't work that way! It doesn't take from one person to give to another.

If you ask for $1,000 you're going to get it. But this thousand dollars is not being taken from another person so that it can be given to you. The creative force behind cosmonomics develops a new source from which your prosperity will come to you. So lay any qualms aside and take another step forward to the realization of your every dream.

HOW TO STRENGTHEN YOUR
UNIVERSAL COSMONOMIC POWER

There is an old saying that, "What you don't use, you lose." This bit of folk wisdom has a great deal of merit.

Very few of you practice lifting weights every day—but you do have the muscles available to lift the weights if you want to. Lifting weights requires that you use muscles that are used little in your usual work-a-day world. You lift the weights, but do you have sore muscles the next day? Sure you do! But if you set up a regular routine of weight lifting, the sore muscles are soon replaced by strong and active muscle that is immune to stress and pain. You have used the muscles and they have responded to your demands in a positive manner.

Cosmonomic power reacts to your demands upon it in much the same manner as weight lifting. The peak of your professional cosmonomic skill is achieved when you use it. The more you use this awesome power the stronger it becomes.

DEVELOP THE ART OF OBSERVATION

You would be surprised at the number of people that ask for a cosmonomic miracle and then fail to recognize it when it is ready to manifest itself in their lives.

The most recent example of this failure of observation concerns a friend of mine. Don T. wanted $900 to buy a kit of supplies so that he could convert the inside of his automobile van into a miniature palace on wheels—much as he had seen demonstrated at the motor van show at the county fairgrounds.

He did most of the right things. He wrote in his notebook what he wanted and why he wanted it. He told his subconscious mind to work a miracle, and the miracle did occur; but, Don let the miracle slip right through his fingers. Here's exactly what happened.

The day after Don affirmed that he wanted and needed $900, he stopped at the grocery store to pick up a loaf of bread on his way home from work. As he passed through the checkout line, the clerk offered him a free chance on the "Super Saver Sweepstake" that was being conducted by the grocery chain. Don brushed the offer aside and headed toward the door. Just as he touched the door to leave he heard a woman screaming. Turning around, Don watched as the lady jumped up and down throwing her arms wildly about. Why was the woman acting in an almost hysterical manner? She was deliriously happy. The sweepstake ticket that Don had refused was handed to her. When she scratched loose the paper concealing the numbers upon her ticket and matched it to the numbers on the sweepstakes board, she had won $1,000. Obviously Don didn't intentionally throw away a thousand dollars, but intentional or not, he did fail to observe what was going on around him and in just a few seconds threw hundreds of dollars away—dollars that were meant for him.

Most people miss about half of their heart's desires because they don't observe what they think they see, don't hear what they think they hear, or don't feel what they think they feel. If what I'm saying doesn't sound realistic, listen to three disinterested witnesses to an automobile accident. Generally you'd believe that they were talking about three different accidents rather than the same one. Or, hand three people an identical simple object and ask them to describe it in detail—for example, a pair of scissors. You won't believe that the three people involved in the experiment are describing the very same object.

Practice! It will be well worth your while. As your ability to observe the world around you increases, so will your ability to work positive cosmonomic miracles. Be constantly alert and in touch with the world around you. Though your miracles originate in another dimension, they manifest themselves in this dimension.

Don't make the same mistake that Don did. Don't lose a miracle by failing to observe that it's right at your fingertips.

Cosmonomics is a creative function that works smoothly and efficiently. It will not step out and hit you on the shoulder to grab your attention. Cosmonomics creates the miracle. It's up to you to accept the miracle.

THE RITUAL THAT WILL BUILD YOUR SEVEN COSMONOMIC ENERGY CENTERS

There are seven major energy centers within the human body. It is from these cosmonomic energy centers that you transmit your own miraculous power into the universe. You transmit your energy signal and the Great Cosmic Mind responds in kind.

Your psychic transmission is the request for the miracle; the response from the Infinite is the manifestation of the miracle.

Each of the seven cosmonomic energy centers controls a specific operation in your life, but all seven centers must be active as you begin your adventure into universal cosmonomics. Your concentration must be upon the total cooperation of all seven energy centers working in unison. Don't be concerned with the specific operation of each individual energy center.

HOW TO BEGIN YOUR MAGIC RITUAL

Begin your cosmonomic ritual by seating yourself in a comfortable chair. Keep your spine erect and rest your hands upon your knees with palms turned upward and feet flat upon the floor.

With eyelids gently closed, visualize a throbbing, pulsating light at the base of your spine. As this energy center acquires a bluish hue, move your mind to your solar plexis and mentally visualize your second cosmonomic energy center. When this has been completed, transfer your thoughts to the area of the heart, followed by the throat area. Now move your concentration to the psychic center which lies behind the bridge of the nose. Now dominate your thoughts by concentrating upon the center of the base of the skull and complete your meditation upon the last of the seven powerful energy centers, which is the center of the head.

When this ritual has been completed, you have made a very definite contact with cosmonomic power. Your life will never again be the same. You can at last be free of the burdens that frustrate attempts at living a healthy, happy, and prosperous life.

HOW TO RECHARGE YOUR
COSMONOMIC BATTERIES

It rarely happens but if, at sometime in the future, you feel your Cosmonomic miracle power slipping, just grab a chair, sit down, relax, and perform the simple ritual that builds the power back into your seven Cosmonomic energy centers.

MAKE SURE THAT YOU REALLY
WANT WHAT YOU'RE ASKING FOR

There are those people who accuse me of advising my students to be overly cautious, and they may have a valid point, but my own experience has shown that people sometimes fail to put the proper miracle into motion. They certainly don't start the wrong forces into motion consciously, but they do put negative forces into play because they fail to be specific when asking for a miracle.

One of my students allowed me to copy this from her notebook:

> I want more love and affection in my life. I want this love and affection because Fred [her husband] is not paying enough attention to me.

Do you see anything wrong with what Velda asked? You probably don't, but this is what happened to Velda.

Within hours of Velda's writing in her notebook, a male friend of longstanding suddenly lost his feelings of just friendship and made every attempt to deluge her with love and affection. Velda was beside herself. She wasn't encouraging her friend's advances, and yet he wouldn't back off. She was upset, her male admirer was upset, and then her husband became furious with jealous anger as he accussed Velda of encouraging what were becoming outrageously public advances toward Velda. Just as Velda believed she was getting one unwanted admirer under control, a second one popped into her life.

Velda had always believed her boss to be a stodgy, moralistic man. In fact, she had secretly believed that he was incapable of experiencing some of the human qualities of life. When Mr. X turned on his charm and advanced toward Velda like a tiger she actually fainted, right on the spot.

It was late at night when my entire household was awakened by Velda's wild pounding at our door.

It took a lot of patience and a lot of time before I could calm the sobbing woman to the point where I could understand what her problem was.

"I thought miracles were supposed to make you happy," she blurted out. "I've never been so miserable in my life. Fred is threating to divorce me, and it's all your fault. I asked for love and affection and I get a divorce! That's no miracle, it's a curse!"

I asked if I could see her notebook.

"You're lucky I even have it," she said as she threw it toward me. One quick glance at Velda's notebook provided the immediate answer to Velda's mysterious problem.

I handed Velda her notebook and asked her to read aloud her miracle request.

"I want more love and affection in my life," she read.

"Now stop right there, Velda," I said. "You asked for more love and affection to enter your life and that's exactly what you got. You didn't say from whom, or in what manner you wanted the attention to come to you."

Obviously Velda meant that she wanted Fred to smother her with love and affection, but that's not what she asked for. She made a false assumption that Universal Cosmonomic Mind was going to correct any errors she might make in requesting a miracle. Cosmonomics teaches that you can and you will perform any miracle you command, but it also places the responsibility squarely upon your own shoulders to make sure you know exactly what you're asking for and that the miracle power, as it manifests within your life, becomes the reality that you truly want it to be. Make sure you want exactly what you're asking for.

HOW SHARON L. USED COSMONOMICS
TO WIN THE MAN SHE LOVED

Unlike Velda in the previous case history, Sharon L. knew exactly what she wanted and whom she wanted it from.

Sharon worked in one of America's largest insurance agencies, but the office in which she worked was dominated by women. Her job left her little time to become acquainted with the hundreds of other male employees that worked outside of her particular accounting area.

"I always had lunch with the girls," she wrote. "The only time I saw any eligible men was in the cafeteria. There wasn't enough time to say hello, let alone become acquainted. The company I worked for was noted for its young, handsome insurance salesmen—and there I was, not even able to get an introduction to one of them.

"There was one man, about forty-five, who I thought was the most handsome man I had ever seen. It was love at first sight on my part, but I couldn't even find out his name. I was really becoming frustrated over the whole affair—I certainly couldn't walk up to him and introduce myself, though I was certainly tempted to do so.

"This may sound strange to you, but I had become so confused over the feelings I felt for this man that I didn't even think about using Cosmonomics to help me out of my mental frustration. I desired that man so much that I felt as if I were being eaten up inside.

"When I really felt the worst, I came across a girl I had met in one of your Cosmonomics classes. Our meeting was brief, but it was long enough to remind me that I had the power to make my dream come true, but hadn't even bothered to use it.

"That night I sat down and wrote out my Cosmonomic plan of action. The first thing I needed to know was if the man were married (I certainly wouldn't want to break up a marriage). No! He wasn't married. 'Good,' I said. 'That's the main hurdle out of the way.' "

Sharon went on to write in her letter that she used her Cosmonomic Power to arrange a chance meeting with the man of her dreams.

"I didn't use my Cosmonomic Power to say how we would meet. I simply stated that I would meet my shining knight on the next Thursday. You'll never believe what happened!

"It was Thursday evening and I was just backing out of my parking place. I was startled when I felt and heard a loud 'crunch.' My dreamboat had backed his car into mine.

"That was two years ago, and it seems as if it were only yesterday. Len, of course, was terribly sorry that he had damaged my car, and he literally insisted that he take me out to dinner as a token of his remorse. I acted nonchalant, but I was ready to explode inside.

"One dinner date led to another and to another. Within six months of the accident, Len and I had an outdoor wedding at his family's estate overlooking the Hudson River. I have a beautiful home, a loving husband, and at this moment I'm expecting twins to add even greater happiness and excitement to my life.

"I've been asked by the few friends I let in on my cosmonomic secret if I really believed Cosmonomics was responsible for my utopian life. I must answer honestly. I have absolutely no doubt that all of my dreams have come true as a direct result of Cosmonomic miracles."

Sharon's story is not an isolated incident, or a coincidence. Before you have completed this book, miracles such as those experienced by Sharon will be an everyday, natural part of your life.

When you use Cosmonomic power don't expect less and don't accept less. Cosmonomics is your magic wand to bring health, wealth, love, security, and happiness to you and to others.

COMMON SENSE WILL IMPROVE YOUR COSMONOMIC POWER PERFORMANCE

The miracle power of Cosmonomics lies within the great Universal Mind, and it is *you* that act as the catalyst to put the Ultra-Cosmonomic to work.

It is easy to perform a Cosmonomic miracle, but you can make it very difficult if you fail to use a little common sense along with your miracle power. Many people do not use their common sense or natural intuitive ability and then question why their miracle power wasn't as successful as they wanted it to be.

If you want love and affection, you obviously must meet people. Performing a Cosmonomic ritual to bring love into your life will just not work if you perform your ritual and then lock yourself in a bomb shelter, sealed off from the world.

Wanda C. needed some money. She knew that the best chance that she had to get money fast was to bet on the horses. On the morning of the race, Wanda picked her horses from those that were listed on the sports page of the newspaper. Eight of the ten horses she picked came in as winners, but Wanda didn't go to the track to place her bets. Obviously, you can't win money from a horse race if you don't bet on the horses.

"I would never do that!" you're probably saying at this very moment. I hope you're right, but I have had communications from hundreds of people just like Wanda. Universal Cosmonomic power does not mean you toss out your own good sense. If you were not to use your own common sense, Cosmic Mind would never have given it to you in the first place.

COSMONOMIC CHARACTERISTICS THAT SHOULD BE INCORPORATED INTO YOUR DAILY LIFE

Cosmonomics teaches that no life is totally under the control of its owner, but that the portion of your life that is controllable should be used to build defenses against bad luck, poverty, disease, loneliness, etc. And the steps that you take to build strong walls against the onslaught of present negativity are quite simple:

1. Become a gregarious individual.

Almost all Cosmonomic miracles are the result of the actions of other people. You win a contest because someone else sponsored the contest. You gain the love and affection you desire because someone else has entered your life who is capable of giving you the required amount of love. Because so many of your miracles are dependent upon the actions of others, you should acquire as many friends and acquaintances as possible. You want everyone possible to know you as a friendly, magnetic person. Develop this simple Cosmonomic characteristic and you will soon discover that people will seek you out and literally beg you to let them do you a favor.

Your new gregariousness will not only open the door to instant miracles, but it will also lay a solid foundation for future miracles that are still to come.

2. Pay attention to your hunches.

A hunch is a conclusion that has not been based upon conscious facts, but the most successful individuals have gone against the deductions of their conscious mind and followed the inner, instinctive urgings of the subconscious mind.

J. Paul Getty created a fortune in oil, Conrad Hilton made millions when he followed his hunches in building his worldwide chain of hotels, and it took more than just the business facts at hand for a manufacturer of time keeping and accounting machines to become the computer giant of the world and one of the most successful corporations in the history of mankind.

3. Don't confuse a hunch with wishful thinking.

Fortunes have been made by following a hunch, but fortunes have also been lost. The fortunes lost were not the result of following a hunch, but the result of mistaking wishful thinking as an instinctive psychic urge.

A very fine line divides the hunch from wishful thinking, but you need not experience this frustration.

Several chapters within this book give detailed instruction on how to discern the difference between a hunch and fanciful hopes, but as a beginner in Cosmonomics, the easiest method would be to consult your prophetic dominos in Chapter Two or your magic deck of cards in Chapter Seven.

4. Don't be timid.

The miracle workers throughout history have had one common characteristic—they have had a sense of boldness. Yes, they have been humble in nature, but they have not been timid by any means. They knew what they wanted and they got it—and you are going to do the very same thing.

Don't be afraid to try something new and don't become set in your ways. When a miracle presents itself, be ready to zigzag or to jump off into a new direction. Be willing to meet your miracle at least half way.

5. Sometimes expect to lose.

I'm promising you miracles in one paragraph and telling you to expect to be a loser in the next. This appears to be a contradiction, but only to your physical nature. Your metaphysical, or higher nature, recognizes that this is an example of cosmic cooperation rather than a human contradiction.

There are many things in your life that are not needed. Things that are in the way, things that are obstructing the performance of your Cosmonomic miracles. Your human natures rebel against losing anything, but there are times when people, objects or attitudes must be removed from your life so that there is room for your miracles to maneuver.

Let's return again to the life of J.P. Getty.

Mr. Getty was attending college and had the strong desire to enter the diplomatic corps—but he also had the desire to go to work at the wildcat oil fields. Obviously he could not do both. He gave up his plush existence at the University and what would have been a certain opportunity of landing an assignment in the diplomatic corps. You might say he lost all of his opportunities. He did lose them in a sense, but what he lost was replaced by something greater and better.

J. Paul Getty left college and worked the oil fields from dawn to dusk. Did J. Paul really lose anything by leaving college? He didn't think so. At the age of 23 he had founded his fortune in oil.

Losses are only an illusion, and in almost every instance are a necessary part of positive miracle power. If at anytime you become upset by an illusory loss, remember these two very important Cosmonomic principles:

- Nothing that really belongs to you can ever be taken from you, and
- Nothing is ever taken from you unless it is to be replaced by something better.

6. Don't be afraid to admit that you made a mistake.

Let's face it! All of us are less than perfect and of course we make errors in judgment. You'll probably make a mistake at one time or another in performing a miracle. You'll find that when you got what you asked for, you really didn't want it.

A personal friend of mine was one of the happiest people I had ever met. He had everything he wanted, and he had a minimum of the frustrations that we all encounter in our everyday worlds.

In some manner, other friends convinced Frank that he should have a big financial nest egg in case he ever needed it. And without even thinking about the consequences, Frank performed a couple of Cosmonomic miracles and had thousands of dollars quickly come his way. Suddenly my peaceful friend was miserable. He had tax problems with the I.R.S., he had friends and family he hadn't seen for years pounding on his door looking for a handout. Finally, he had to move from his dream house into an isolated apartment. His entire life turned from happiness to despair. Frank was the first person to admit that he had made a mistake, and he didn't blame anyone else for his problems.

I received a letter from Frank not long ago. He asked me to pass on the advice of a self-made millionaire who was not afraid to admit that he had made a mistake.

If you are losing a tug-of-war with a tiger, give him the rope before he gets to your arm. You can always buy a new rope.

7. Forget about "Murphy's Law."

It is unfortunate that pessimism can play such an important role in the life of so many, but it does. The person who follows Murphy's Law ("If something can go wrong it will") has already half defeated his own useful purposes. Pessimism leads to demoralization of character that will leave you unable to react to your opportunities in a constructive manner.

Murphy's Law? Toss it out!

DON'T WASTE YOUR NEW FOUND POWERS TRYING TO CONVINCE THE SKEPTIC

It's part of your human nature to want to share a good thing with your fellow mortals, but the whole thing can backfire on you. The first thing you'll discover is that you'll be spending all of your time trying to convince the skeptic and have no time to perform the miracles that will bring you the health, wealth, and happiness that are yours for the asking. The best way to handle a skeptic is to refuse to even discuss Cosmonomics with him. When he sees the changes the Cosmonomic Miracle Power brings into your life he'll soon lose his skepticism and be begging you to share your secrets with him.

I've been dealing with skeptics for over thirty years, and believe me, you're just wasting your Cosmonomic power in attempts to prove your own beliefs. As your fame as a miracle worker spreads, you'll undoubtedly be contacted by newspaper reporters or free-lance writers looking for a story. True, it's flattering, but the publicity can be a blessing or a curse. Once you appear in print, everything you then do is held up for public scrutiny. This is great, but make sure you can handle the consequences that come with new found fame.

I rarely give interviews, but just this past week I was contacted by a reporter from the *San Jose Mercury-News* who wanted to do a story for the "California Today," Sunday supplement. I knew the reporter was struggling to make a name and consented to the interview only because I wanted to do a good turn. The reporter was a wonderful person, but as with all skeptics her first words were, "Before we begin the interview, tell me all about myself." My reply left little doubt where I stood on the matter.

"First of all," I said, "I have absolutely no interest in your personal life or affairs, and secondly I have absolutely no desire to convince you of anything."

The interview did end on a happy and positive note, however. I escorted her through my home to see the material luxury I enjoy, I let her view my rare book collection worth thousands of dollars, I pointed to the luxury auto sitting in the driveway, etc. I then told the reporter of my two successful children, and when I mentioned their ages, she absolutely refused to believe my own age. [Chapter Three explains how you too can look years younger.]

The reporter's parting words were, "My God! I've got to go home and go to bed. This whole thing has just boggled my mind."

YOU CAN CHANGE ANYTHING IN YOUR LIFE IF YOUR TIMING IS RIGHT

Timing has a great deal to do with the successful manifestation of your Cosmonomic miracles. "For everything there is a season," is a literal truth, and this principle must be taken into consideration when you perform your ritual to create a universal Cosmonomic miracle. That Great Universal Intelligence that works in and through all things knows that all things must be done in a proper sequential order before there can be the perfect manifestation of your heart's desire.

There will be times when you will demand an "instant" miracle and it will not instantly occur, but the miracle you request *will* occur at the proper time, in the proper way, and at the proper place.

Helen R. was a wealthy woman whose financial affairs were closely entwined with her husband's through joint ownership of companies, stocks, bonds and other financial instruments.

Helen and Ken's marriage had not been one of love and never would be. The marriage was consummated solely as a social and financial convenience. As the years passed, Helen grew to hate her husband and began to yearn for a husband to enable her to bask in a warm glow of love and affection. Helen performed her ritual to capture a mate and he appeared promptly on the scene. Now common sense should have told Helen to untangle herself from her present husband's financial saddle before she sought a new mate. Helen asked for things out of sequence and wound up a loser.

A lengthy, messy, and costly divorce proceeding dragged on and on. By the time a court settlement was reached, Helen's lover tired of the constant conflict and moved to another area. Helen's lack of timing made a mess of her life. Don't make the same type of mistake as Helen. Do your part in assuring that your miracle happens at the right time.

HOW NELSON E. BORROWED $3,000 AND TURNED IT INTO $40,000 WITHIN SIX MONTHS

This true case history of Nelson E. shows you what you can expect to be happening to you long before you have read half-way through this book.

Nelson E. was a printer by trade. He had no savings, but he did lead a comfortable life. The only thing that he wanted that he already didn't have was $40,000 to build a new house for his elderly parents.

"Mom and Dad were up in years," he told me one evening. "They had a house, but there were a lot of stairs that they had to go up and down. Both of them had arthritis, and the constant up and down the stairs was a very painful experience for them. They lived in the country and got lonesome. They weren't able to get out enough to visit their friends as they would have liked."

Nelson continued telling me of the hopes he had had of providing a modern kitchen for his mother and a workshop for his Dad.

"You certainly lacked any selfish motives," I said. "Did you perform a Cosmonomic miracle and get the money you wanted?"

Nelson admitted that he had at first been skeptical, but he had made up his mind to give Cosmonomics a try.

Several months passed before I heard of Nelson again, but what I did hear the following December made me very happy.

On the very night that Nelson performed his first ritual for financial prosperity he had a strange dream about coffee beans. He had the same recurrent dream for weeks before he realized what his dream meant. He thought the dream meant that he was to invest money in a "coffee farm."

Nelson knew absolutely nothing about the commodities market, but he did visit a broker. The broker was a kindly man and explained to Nelson that you didn't buy stock in a "coffee farm," but invested in what were called "coffee futures" on the Exchange.

Against the advice of the broker, Nelson insisted that the $3,000 he had borrowed from his boss be invested in coffee futures. "When my coffee's worth $43,000 call me," Nelson told the astonished financial expert.

If you recall what happened to the price of coffee during 1976, you can well realize how Nelson made a $40,000 profit in such a short time.

Let me assure you, Nelson E. is not an isolated case of one person successfully using the universal power of Cosmonomics. He is but one of many who have discovered for themselves that this awesome Cosmonomic miracle power is not a whimsical occult fantasy, but a very real creative force that is now waiting to take you on the most exciting adventure of your life—an adventure of love, happiness, good health, and riches that yesterday seemed a dream. Today, all of these rich rewards are yours for the asking. Read on and let *Universal Mind* prove what it has to offer, just for you.

Chapter Two

HOW DOMINOS BRING YOU LOVE AND PROSPERITY THROUGH A MYSTIC UNIVERSAL MIND CODE

Cosmic Mind speaks to you in many different ways, but none is more startling than the cosmic code concealed in an ordinary set of dominos. Dominos will give visible evidence that Cosmic Mind is in touch with the future. Cosmic Mind knows the future and is ready to reveal its secrets to you.

Dominos are but one of the many unique tools that can be used to foretell the future. This divining tool of Universal Cosmonomics will lead you to constant happiness, love, and prosperity.

A SET OF DOMINOS CAN ANSWER
YOUR EVERY QUESTION

There are times within your life when you doubt the impressions of your own mind. Are you really foretelling the future or is your mind playing tricks? Are your visions of the future simply wishful thinking?

Dominos remove the doubt. Their spots and dots are a secret code that spells out exactly what the future holds. And if you don't like what the future holds, you have ample opportunity to turn the future around by using the occult techniques found in later chapters of this book.

THE ANCIENT CHINESE WERE THE
FIRST TO USE DOMINOS

Dominos, in the Western world, are of fairly recent origin. It has only been during the last two hundred years that dominos, as a game, gained popularity in Europe. Divining the future with dominos is done by a mere handful of psychic followers in the Western world. Millions of others look upon dominos as merely a game—missing entirely the mystical significance of the dots upon the rectangular blocks.

It was thousands of years ago that the ancient Chinese developed dominos as a fortune telling tool. The dots, or spots, upon today's domino remain exactly as they did in ancient China. But the ancient Chinese designed beautifully intricate pictures and designs upon the faces of their dominos in addition to the spots or dots we are familiar with today.

Though today's domino does not bear beautifully designed pictures, the spots upon the domino remain the same as in ancient China. And it is the secret coding and spacing of the dots upon the dominos that allows Cosmic Mind to whisper secrets of the future into your ear.

THE CODED DOTS SPEAK TO EVERY MAN

Cosmic Mind does not play favorites. The secret coding of the dots upon the blocks reveals the future to any person who wants to take the time to read them. But in divining the future through dominos, you do become a unique individual. There are very, very few people familiar with the mystical domino Cosmonomic code.

HOW DOMINOS POINT TO FUTURE EVENTS

Each domino within the set has a mystical meaning. Its Cosmonomic code points to events that will soon appear in your future. They will answer your every question.

The dominos can be consulted about your future hopes and dreams, and with their guidance, your dreams can become realities.

Since the introduction of dominos into the Western world, two schools of thought have developed. The Western school has developed new and sometimes different interpretations as to the cosmic code upon the domino.

The Eastern school relies upon the code as interpreted by the ancient Chinese soothsayer. Though I personally prefer the ancient mystical interpretations, I will reveal both the ancient and modern codes.

DOMINOS FORETELL, THEY DO NOT COMPEL

At various points within this book I will remind you that your psychic tools are revealing the trends of the future and the future conceivable outcome. They are not compelling you to accept the future.

If your fortune telling tool reveals a future that is of your liking, continue your life as it is. If an unhappy future is foretold, you have ample opportunity to turn it around so that the future gives only happiness, health, and prosperity.

HOW TO ACQUIRE YOUR DOMINOS

Dominos can be made of ebony, plastic, wood, or a number of other substances. The material that they are constructed of makes no difference in fortune telling power. Dominos are ordinarily black, with white dots. But on occasion, dominos with the colors reversed can be purchased—white blocks with black dots.

These dominos that are reversed in color (white with black spots) are the favorites of the domino diviner. But these white dominos possess no more divining power than the usual inexpensive black dominos—it is simply a matter of personal preference.

Dominos can be purchased at any toy counter. The price you pay and the quality of workmanship have no significance when you begin to foretell the future with your own set of dominos.

If, at a later time, you discover that divining the future with dominos will be your regular routine, a more expensive set of dominos can be easily acquired.

My own set of dominos are ivory with ebony dots—but they were a gift from a famous author for whom I had read the dominos. For years I had been very content and successful in using a set of black dominos that cost less than a dollar.

THE RITUAL THAT WILL ATTUNE
YOU TO THE SECRET COSMIC CODE

After purchasing your dominos, take them home and remove them from their container.

Place the dominos face down upon a table, and begin stirring them with your right hand. The stirring motion should always be to the right, or clockwise. Continue stirring for approximately two minutes.

The remainder of the ritual is very important. And though it may appear repetitious, it is absolutely essential that it be followed exactly in the manner that I will reveal to you.

After the dominos have been stirred throughly, pick up one domino with your right hand. Transfer the domino to your left hand. During the transfer, speak these words:

I dedicate this block to Cosmic Mind. It will forever speak
the truth to all who seek its prophetic power.

Perform this ritual with each domino, placing them in a neat pile on your left. When the ritual has been completed, your divining dominos are ready to speak to you in their unique, prophetic, Cosmonomic code.

HOW TO CARE FORYOUR DOMINOS

Your dominos need no special care, but they should be reserved for divining purposes only. They should never be used for the playing of any domino game if they are to be used for divining.

One lady became very distraught when it became obvious that her divining dominos were uttering false prophecies. She could find no explanation for the sudden turn of events. Her dominos had gained a reputation for truth and accuracy and suddenly they were speaking with a "forked tongue."

After much investigation, the diviner discovered that her children had been using her divining blocks to play games during her absence. A new set of dominos placed out of reach of her children soon restored the reputation for truthfulness from her prophetic dominos.

HOW THE DIVINING DOMINOS LED GEORGE M.
TO A RICH AND SUCCESSFUL LIFE

George M. was one of those unfortunate people who seem to have consistently bad luck. It seemed that no matter what he did or how honorable his motives were, nothing especially good seemed to come his way.

George became more and more discouraged as he watched people with much less talent than he soar to success.

George was a Certified Public Accountant, and he was a good one. But his real interest lay in writing.

George wasn't destitute, but he only made enough money to furnish his family with the bare essentials. There was never enough left for the extra luxuries that most of his friends enjoyed.

"I was having some minor success in writing," George told me, "but I had given up any hope of making a good living from writing. I was receiving rejection slip after rejection slip."

It was at one of George's lowest emotional periods that he became acquainted with a domino diviner.

"All writers have an inquisitive mind," George later said, "and I really didn't think the future could be foretold with dominos. But I was interested in the story behind the dominos, and I was interested as to why Madge [the domino diviner] believed the dots on the face of the dominos."

The budding writer thought that a story on domino fortune telling might make for a good magazine article—and it did. But during his research for the article he discovered that Madge's dominos were predicting his future with uncanny accuracy. It was at this time that George decided to consult the dominos on a story idea that he had been carrying around in his head.

"I had what I thought was a good story plot, but I just couldn't get it down on paper. I had tried for two years to work my plot into a novel, but I couldn't make it jell together."

George continued. "The dominos were so darned accurate on foretelling the future that I decided to see if they could help me develop my novel.

"I had the first chapter written when I consulted the dominos on the theme that I should carry into the second chapter. When I finished writing the second chapter, I asked the advice of the dominos on the third, and then the fourth. Before I knew it, my novel was complete."

George M. is a fictitious name, but this case history is absolutely true.

HOW TO USE YOUR DOMINOS TO
FORETELL THE FUTURE

Most domino diviners prefer to place a piece of velvet upon the table before them. Then upon the velvet, the diviner places the dominos face down and stirs them thoroughly with the right hand.

PRONOUNCE THE MAGIC WORD
AS YOU STIR THE DOMINOS

While you, the diviner, stir the dominos, you must declare the magic word that will make the dominos answer the question that your client is asking. The magic word is your client's first name spelled backward, plus two additional rules.

1. After the name has been spelled backward, a letter *e* is placed between any two consonants.
2. After the name has been spelled backward, a letter *e* is added as the last letter.

Here are examples showing you how to make your magic word.

Robert is the name of your client.

Robert spelled backward is *Trebor*.

Now add the letter e between the consonants (*t* and *r*), an *e* at the end of the name, and your magic word is *Te-re-bo-re*.

Here are other examples. It is very easy and can be done quickly once you get the hang of it.

Betty = Ytteb

Now add the *e* between the *y* and *t*, and then the two *t's* and you have *Yeteteb*. Add the *e* at the end of the word, and your magic word is *Ye-te-te-be*.

Name	Name Reversed	Name with Letter "E" Added	Magic Word
CARL	= LRAC	LERACE	LE-RA-CE
DAVID	= DIVAD	DIVADE	DI-VA-DE
CARRIE	= EIRRAC	EIRERACE	EI-RE-RA-CE
DONALD	= DLANOD	DELANODE	DE-LA-NO-DE
WALTER	= RETLAW	RETELAWE	RE-TE-LA-WE
MAUDIE	= EIDUAM	EIDUAME	EI-DU-AM-E
CINDY	= YDNIC	YEDENICE	YE-DE-NI-CE
VELMA	= AMLEV	AMELEVE	AM-EL-EV-E

The procedure to find your magic word is simple and takes but a few seconds of your time. If you do not use the magic word, the advice given by your dominos will remain questionable at best.

If you will be giving readings about the future to a large number of people, you can keep a listing of your magic words in a small notebook. This will save you a great deal of time when a client is sitting across the table waiting for you to divine the future.

THE ONE DOMINO DRAW

Your dominos have been stirred and you've pronounced the magic word over them. Your client should now draw one domino with his left hand and turn it face up upon the table. This domino will reveal what will happen in his life during the next week.

THE DIVINER MAY NOT DRAW A DOMINO
TO FORECAST HIS OWN FUTURE

Dominos are the only fortune telling device where the diviner must rely upon a second person before he can divine his own future.

If you wish to divine your own future with the dominos, you must ask another person to draw the domino for you.

Legend tells that any domino diviner drawing his own domino from the pile will suffer twelve months of bad luck.

HOW TO READ THE CODE
OF THE ONE DOMINO DRAW

It is for the domino diviner to decide if he will follow the Eastern, or the Western interpretation of the coded spots upon the domino in the one domino draw.

Most diviners use the Eastern method of interpretation, but those following the Western method have also shown startling accuracy. I would suggest that you use the method that you feel the most comfortable with. For convenience sake, I have listed both the Eastern and the Western interpretation of the domino's cosmic code.

HOW TO READ THE COSMIC CODE
(THE EASTERN METHOD)

The Eastern method of reading the cosmic code uses the entire set of dominos, with each domino having its own unique and individual message.

This one domino draw tells what can be expected to happen in the coming week. It is unlucky to make another domino draw during that one week period.

Domino Drawn	Cosmic Code Interpretation
Double-blank	Life will be uneventful and dull.
Double-one	An advantageous discovery will take place out-of-doors.
One-blank	You will be scorned after a rash decision.
One-two	You will mortgage or borrow money on a piece of property.
One-three	You will be startled by a new discovery.
One-four	Debts will worry you. Do not undertake new financial obligations.
One-five	A love affair.
One-six	You help an old friend.
Double-two	Your life is clouded by jealousy.
Two-blank	An irritating delay that will leave shortly.
Two-one	You will mortgage or borrow money on a piece of property.
Two-three	Avoid gambling or games of chance. You will lose.
Two-four	Your fortunes begin an unexpected upturn.
Two-five	An outing on the water.
Two-six	You receive a gift of clothing.
Double-three	You will be annoyed by an unexpected wedding.
Three-blank	An illegitimate child enters your life.

Domino Drawn	Cosmic Code Interpretation
Three-one	You will be startled by a new discovery.
Three-two	Avoid gambling or games of chance. You will lose.
Three-four	You will meet a former sweetheart.
Three-five	An agreeable change in your work.
Three-six	A visit to a theater or the arts.
Double-four	A happy weekend away from home.
Four-blank	Ignore an angry letter.
Four-one	Debts will worry you. Do not undertake new fiinancial obligations.
Four-two	Your fortunes begin to rise.
Four-three	You will meet a former sweetheart.
Four-five	A speculation turns out well.
Four-six	You will play a part in a lawsuit.
Double-five	You will make a sudden move.
Five-blank	A funeral, but not from your own family.
Five-one	A love affair.
Five-two	An outing on the water.
Five-three	An agreeable change in your work.
Five-four	A speculation turns out well.
Five-six	The birth of a child will change your life.
Double-six	Money comes to you unexpectedly.

Domino Drawn	Cosmic Code Interpretation
Six-blank	Scandal is spread by a supposed friend.
Six-one	You help an old friend.
Six-two	You receive a gift of clothing.
Six-three	A visit to the theater or the arts.
Six-four	You will play a part in a lawsuit.
Six-five	The birth of a child will change your life.

HOW TO USE THE WESTERN METHOD
TO READ THE COSMONOMIC CODE

Unlike the Eastern method where all dominos are used to forecast the future, the Western method requires that all dominos with any blanks on them be removed from the set.

When the stirring of the dominos and the pronouncement of the magic word has been completed, one domino is drawn with the left hand.

THE UNLUCKY DOMINOS

There are two unlucky dominos if you are foretelling the future using the Western method of decoding the cosmic secrets. These dominos are Four-Two, which indicates a disappointment, in addition to the general interpretation. The second unlucky domino is the Three-One, which foretells bad news of a temporary kind.

DOMINO DOUBLES HOLD A SPECIAL MEANING

The double dominos have special interpretations that never vary or waiver. It is these double dominos which are considered the lucky dominos.

DOMINO	DOUBLE DOMINO COSMIC CODE
Double-one	A happy journey to an unfamiliar place.
Double-two	New friends and happy times.
Double-three	A new love affair.
Double-four	Unexpected money coming in a very dramatic way.
Double-five	A new job or promotion at your present place of employment.
Double-six	The wedding of the person drawing this domino; or if already married, special good fortune coming from a wedding.

You will notice that "something new" is the keynote of all double dominos.

GENERAL DOMINO INTERPRETATIONS

Speaking in general, the fortunes cast by the dominos are interpreted according to very inflexible rules.

Sixes — All sixes signify good luck in connection with the wish held in the mind while drawing the domino.

Fives — Refer to work or career.

Fours — Money matters.

Threes — Love affairs.

Twos — Friends and social affairs.

Ones — Journeys and travels.

HOW TO READ THE COSMIC CODES

Domino	Interpretation
One-two	Travel with friends.
One-three	Travel with or to a lover.
One-four	Travel because of work or money matters.

Domino	Interpretation
One-five	Travel due to work or career.
One-six	A wish to travel will come true.
Two-one	Travel with friends.
Two-three	Love affairs between friends.
Two-four	Money coming through friendships.
Two-five	There will be new friends found through work or career.
Two-six	The forging of strong and lasting friendships.
Three-one	Travel with, or to, a lover.
Three-two	Love affairs between friends.
Three-four	Money through romance.
Three-five	Work or career advancement as the result of a love affair.
Three-six	The beginning of a love affair.
Four-one	Travel because of work or money matters.
Four-two	Money coming through friendships.
Four-three	Money through romance.
Four-five	More money through work or career.
Four-six	Unexpected money.
Five-one	Travel due to work or career.
Five-two	New friends will be found at work.
Five-three	Work or career advancement because of a love affair.
Five-four	More money through work or career.
Five-six	Sudden advancement or recognition at work.
Six-one	A wish to travel will come true.
Six-two	The forging of strong and lasting friendships.
Six-three	The beginning of a love affair.
Six-four	Unexpected money.
Six-five	Sudden advancement or recognition at work.

THE FUTURE OF TWO PEOPLE CAN BE FORECAST AT ONE SITTING

As your reputation as a diviner of the dominos spreads, you will probably be inundated by requests to forecast the future. Under these circumstances, the only method that can be used to cut down the requests upon your time is to divine for two people at the same time—two people, never more. Attempting to foretell the future for more than two people at a time can lead to disastrously incorrect predictions.

BOTH PERSONS MUST STIR THE DOMINOS

If you are going to read the dominos for two people at the same time, both parties must stir the dominos. After the dominos have been stirred, you must then utter the magic word for both parties over the dominos. It makes no difference as to which magic word (your clients' names spelled backward), you pronounce first. It is, however, necessary that the first draw be made by the person whose name is first in the alphabet. For example, Betty would draw before Bob, Dave before Norma, Al before Mike, Eileen before Mary, etc.

As the domino diviner, you must make certain that all domino draws are done with the left hand. If a domino is mistakenly drawn with the right hand, no interpretation should be attempted at that sitting. The person incorrectly drawing the domino with the right hand should not be given another domino reading until a full seven days has passed.

HOW TO FORECAST THE FUTURE
FOR A FULL YEAR

One week forecasts are extremely beneficial, but you will want to know the future for the next twelve month period of time. This full year forecast can be done very simply if the instructions that I reveal to you are followed completely. In divining by dominos, there is no short cut.

After a full year forecast has been completed, it is still proper to continue with the one domino, one week forecasts that I have explained earlier in this chapter.

THE ASTROLOGICAL TWELVE DOMINO DRAW

The one year forecast begins in the same manner as the one domino draw. Your client stirs the dominos with the right hand as you prounounce the magic word. Your client now begins to draw twelve dominos, one at a time, with the left hand. Each domino drawn will relate to the most important event that will take place in each astrological month of the coming year.

The first domino drawn represents the astrological sign under which your client was born. This first domino foretells the most outstanding event that will occur during your client's birthday month of the coming year.

The second domino drawn predicts the events of the month following the birthday month. Sound a bit complicated? It really isn't at all. Just refer to the The Astrological Forecast table.

Your client's birthday is November 4th. Her first domino draw rests upon Scorpio. Her second draw rests upon Sagittarius, her third upon Capricorn, her fourth draw upon Aquarius, the fifth domino rests upon Pisces. The next domino drawn is for Aires, then Taurus, etc. You now have the cosmic code before you for a full year forecast.

HOW TO INTERPRET THE
ASTROLOGICAL FORECAST

The first domino drawn rests upon the birth sign of your client, but this is not the first domino read.

Your interpretation of the domino's cosmic code begins with the astrological sign prevalent at the time of the reading. If, for example, you are reading the domino on May 3rd, the first domino to be read is Taurus. The reading then progresses through the remaining eleven months of the coming year.

The Astrological Forecast

Mar 21	April 20	May 21	Jun 22	Jul 22	Aug 22
Apr 19	May 20	Jun 21	Jul 21	Aug 21	Sep 22
Aries	**Taurus**	**Gemini**	**Cancer**	**Leo**	**Virgo**

Sep 23	Oct 23	Nov 22	Dec 22	Jan 21	Feb 20
Oct 22	Nov 21	Dec 21	Jan 20	Feb 19	Mar 20
Libra	**Scorpio**	**Sagittarius**	**Capricorn**	**Aquarius**	**Pisces**

WEAVE THE COSMIC CODE INTO A STORY

All codes are short and cryptic—right to the point. The cosmic code is no exception to this rule.

As you begin reading the dominos for a full year forecast, weave their message into a story. The person for whom you are forecasting will want much more than what, to them might sound to be "canned" statements. The message from one domino leads to the next domino, and then to the next. The entire year of predictions should be given as one long story rather than as just twelve separate statements.

THE TWELVE DOMINO ASTROLOGICAL COSMIC CODE

The entire set of dominos must be used to predict a one year forecast. The blank dominos are essential in achieving accurate prophecies for a full year. The astrological dominos are interpretated in this manner:

DOMINO DRAWN	ASTROLOGICAL CODE INTERPRETATION
Double blank	Deep and intense negativity. Expect the worst, for it will surely happen. Avoid travel by air and by water. Do not make binding commitments. Do not marry during this month. Ruin looms upon the horizon. Be conservative.
One-blank	The news that you have waited for arrives. Many happy tidings. New and beneficial friendships. Women with dark hair will rule this month.
Double-one	New and interesting pursuits. New knowledge or education upon a new and exciting subject. You will visit the theater or meet actors and actresses.
One-two	You will go begging for what you will need des-

DOMINO DRAWN	ASTROLOGICAL CODE INTERPRETATION
	perately. Old friends may leave, but new friends will soon be found.
One-three	A happy surprise is on the way.
One-four	Trouble through debts. Do not begin new financial obligations. Do not buy or sell property.
One-five	A romance or love affair. Blue eyes rule this month.
One-six	You will need help from a friend. Don't hesitate to ask for advice from a trusted companion.
Two-blank	A month of minor but annoying difficulties.
Double-two	Do not let jealousy hinder your progress. Do not answer criticism from a trusted relative.
Two-one	You will go begging for what is desperately needed. Old friends may leave, but new friends will soon appear.
Two-three	You will lose in financial speculations.
Two-four	There will be loss by theft. Quick action can capture the thief.
Two-five	A month for parties and new friends. Look up old friends. A school chum may appear during this month. Blond hair, dark eyes, rule this month.
Two-six	New clothes. Happy changes. More money.

DOMINO DRAWN	ASTROLOGICAL CODE INTERPRETATION
Three-blank	Surprises from young people. They are correct. Let them make own decisions.
Double-three	A marriage or binding contract.
Three-one	A happy surprise is on the way.
Three-two	You will lose in financial speculation.
Three-four	Troubles in the home.
Three-five	An unexpected visitor. A pleasant experience if handled tenderly.
Three-six	Travel will be slow. Wait until another time. Postpone vacation.
Four-blank	Annoying but important communications.
Double-four	A happy and peaceful month.
Four-one	Trouble through debts. Do not begin new financial obligations. Do not buy or sell property.
Four-two	There will be loss by theft. Quick action can capture villain.
Four-three	Troubles in the home.
Four-five	Good luck in speculation
Four-six	A gift of money, or winning a lawsuit.
Five-blank	Sorrow, but not in your own home.
Double-five	A new house or home.
Five-one	A romance or love affair. Blue eyes rule this month.
Five-two	A month for parties and making new friends. Look

DOMINO DRAWN	ASTROLOGICAL CODE INTERPRETATION
	up old friends. A school chum may appear during this month. Blond hair, dark eyes rule this month.
Five-three	An unexpected visitor. A pleasant experience if handled tenderly.
Five-four	Good luck in speculation.
Five-six	Attendance at a public or formal occasion.
Six-blank	Be cautious. Time is on your side.
Double-six	Money is on the way.
Six-one	You will need help from a friend. Accept advice from a trusted companion.
Six-two	New clothes. Happy changes. More money.
Six-three	Travel will be slow. Wait until another time. Postpone vacation.
Six-four	A gift of money, or winning a lawsuit.
Six-five	Attendance at a public, or formal occassion.

IF YOU DON'T LIKE THE FUTURE, CHANGE IT!

There are hundreds of obvious reasons why divining by dominos is a practical matter. The one week or the twelve month forecast allows you to know the future and to react to this future in a positive manner.

If the predictions from the dominos are positive, continue on your present course. "What if the dominos show bad fortunes?" you may ask.

Knowing the negative influences that might be before you allows you to react to these negative forces and to change them.

Change them so that they are positive influences and make them work for your good fortune.

The remaining chapters of this book give you explicit and detailed instructions on how to make your present and your future one of happiness and plenty—how to wash away bad news and replace it with joyous good news. Don't expect anything less than the best, and don't accept less than the best. This book will help to carry you over any hurdle that might be forecast for your future.

Divining by dominos is truthful and amazingly accurate. Chapter seven of this book reveals an additional Cosmic Code that will enhance the present as you understand the future. But don't jump ahead in the book. The chapters have been developed in a particular sequence—a sequence that reveals the entire Miracle of Universal Mind.

Chapter 3

UNIVERSAL MEDI-COSMONOMIC FINGER PRESSURE CAN BRING YOU PERFECT HEALTH

The best cure for any illness is to prevent the sickness from occurring in the first place. And this is exactly what Medi-Cosmonomic Finger Pressure is all about—the prevention of illness before it happens. But if illness does occur, finger pressure can offer the cure.

If you are presently ill or your friends or family are presently suffering an affliction, this chapter will teach you an ancient occult healing technique. If you are presently in good health, this chapter is still written for you. Medi-Cosmonomic Finger Pressure reveals how you can maintain your good health, vigor, and vitality.

COSMIC FINGER PRESSURE CAN EITHER CURE
OR PREVENT AN ILLNESS

If you, your friends, or family are already afflicted with pain or illness, the more traditional forms of healing have probably already been tried—as well they should.

Once an illness or disease has begun to wrack the body, the sufferer should not neglect the opinions of competent medical doctors. Medical science can perform wonders, and really, once an illness is upon you it makes little difference how it is cured—whether it be by occult methods or by medical science.

In my previous book, *Psychic Telemetry*[1], I outlined many successful forms of occult healing. But it is in this book that Medi-Cosmonomic Finger Pressure is taught as an improved healing tool. This chapter also reveals how you can learn to use this powerful psychic force as a method to prevent illness before it even begins.

COSMIC FINGER PRESSURE HAS BEEN PRACTICED
SINCE THE DAWN OF HUMANITY

When a part of the body is sluggish or in pain, the natural reaction is to press or rub it with the fingers and hands. And this is probably the origin of Cosmonomic Finger Pressure.

Finger pressure was originally a purely Japanese technique, and those practitioners of the art in today's Japan claim that finger pressure was practiced centuries earlier than the more popular Chinese acupuncture which relies upon needles rather than upon the more simple and more powerful finger pressure of the Japanese.

MEDI-COSMONOMIC FINGER PRESSURE IS NOT MEDICINE

Strictly speaking, finger pressure is not medicine. Cosmonomic Finger Pressure is a primary way to prevent the development of sickness. And it is a method to be used to keep the

---

[1] Robert A. Ferguson *Psychic Telemetry* (West Nyack: Parker Publishing Company, Inc., 1977).

body in top condition so that problems do not arise that might require medical attention.

If the body is not in top condition, Medi-Cosmonomic Finger Therapy will soon restore it to a positive wholeness.

COSMONOMIC FINGER PRESSURE IS SIMPLE

Fundamentally, finger pressure is quite simple. Its power as a preventative and a curative measure relies upon pressure applied by the fingers to specific points upon the human body. This pressure as applied by the fingers stimulates the body's own natural self-curative abilities and thus prevents the onset of illness or disease. If pain or disease wracks the body, finger pressure stimulates the body to rid itself of the unwelcome intruder.

Finger pressure is simple because it can be used anywhere, at any time. The only equipment needed is your own fingers and a patient to work upon. And as your fame as a Cosmonomic Finger Pressure specialist spreads, you will have plenty of patients— probably more than you can efficiently handle.

FINGER PRESSURE THERAPY IS PLEASANT

There are no medicines, injections, or other devices used in Cosmonomic Finger Pressure Therapy. Only the fingers are used, and these cosmic fingers produce feelings of warmth and other pleasant sensations. As no medicine is applied, there are also no unpleasant side effects to be experienced by yourself or your patients.

HOW COSMONOMICS
PREVENTS AND CURES AN ILLNESS

The pressure that you apply to the skin during finger pressure therapy stimulates the body's natural recuperative powers. This stimulation causes the diffusion of toxic materials that accumulates in the tissues, muscles, and blood cells. If the toxic materials are scattered, they cannot create an illness, nor can an illness remain once your Cosmonomic power is applied.

HOW YOU CAN BECOME A COSMONOMIC
FINGER PRESSURE THERAPIST

The first and most important quality that is needed to become a therapist is the simple desire to prevent illness and the desire to abort any attempt by fate to create an illness. But first you must perform the ritual that will put a power in your fingers that almost defies description.

THE POWERFUL RITUAL THAT WILL FILL YOUR
FINGERS WITH COSMIC ENERGY

The secret of Cosmic Finger Pressure, if it be a secret, is the tremendous amount of psychic energy that will pass through your fingertips to the pressure point that you are revitalizing upon the body.

Your therapy should begin in a quiet and relaxed atmosphere that is conducive to a quiet and peaceful mind.

When your mind is quiet and clear of the cares of the day, sit in an armless straight-backed chair. While still in this position, repeat these words:

> I attune myself with the Infinite Cosmic Mind, and in this attunement I implore that my fingers be filled with powerful cosmic energy.

> I will use my power only for good. I will destroy all things that can poison the mind and the body and keep all things healthy and whole.

You should now raise both hands to shoulder level, with your fingers pointing upward to the sky. And with conviction, you should now say:

> My fingers are filled with power *Now!*

This ritual should be performed only once. Its power will remain with you for as long as you use it as therapy to cure or prevent pain and illness.

It is not an unusual condition where the rays of energy extending from your fingers will be clearly visible to the physical eye. These cosmic rays can be compared most closely to the soft beam of light reflected from a flashlight with weak batteries.

These energy rays will extend from all fingers, but the greatest power will pour from the thumb and index finger—the fingers that you will use most often in your Cosmic Finger Pressure Therapy.

HOW TO TEST YOUR NEW FOUND
COSMIC POWER

If Cosmic Finger Pressure is not used to cure a disease how can there be any evaluation of its effectiveness? Two recent case histories of finger therapy have come to my attention that afforded the cosmic therapist the opportunity of proving the effectiveness of her finger pressure technique. The first case concerns a middle-aged man that had for years suffered the pain of migraine headaches.

COSMIC FINGER PRESSURE
LEFT ROBERT F. PAIN FREE

Robert F. had visited Mona several times before he learned of her unique healing power. Robert felt his future was to be filled with negative illness because of the continuing debilitating effects of the migraine headaches he had suffered from for years. Mona suggested that Robert undergo once-a-week Cosmic Finger Pressure Therapy.

Before the therapy began, Robert was bedridden at least once a week with his excruciating head pain. He has now been undergoing finger therapy for one full year—and he has not had one headache in that entire period of time. Was a disease cured in Robert's case? How else could this cure be explained? Medi-Cosmonomic Power did the necessary work needed to restore Robert to health.

Migraine headaches are not a disease. Medical science knows little of their causes or their cures. But it is known that something within the system kicks off the headache.

Mona did not use her cosmic therapy at a time when Robert was laid low with pain. Her efforts would have had little effect upon him because of his negative attitude. She began the therapy between headaches—at a time that Robert was not undergoing pain or suffering from a migrane. Mona did not cure the migraine. What she did was neutralize whatever that something was that caused the migraine before it could trigger pain.

Working with migraine sufferers gives you the chance to make a positive test of your new powers to prevent pain or disease.

THE CURIOUS CASE OF BETTY B.'S ARTHRITIS

Betty B. was an employee in the county's tax office. Her job required her to personally visit businesses within the county. It was a good job and Betty liked it—at least until a crippling type arthritis began to develop in her right knee.

"There were times I almost found it impossible to get in and out of the car to pay my calls," Betty said. "The arthritis was strange," she continued. "There were days when I would have very little pain, or none at all. And then there would be days when I could hardly stand on my right leg. At times it became necessary to use a cane during my arthritis flare-ups.

"Injections of cortison administered by a medical doctor were ineffective. I was finally told to take aspirin and bear the pain the best that I could."

It was at this point that Betty B. came in contact with a finger pressure therapist.

The cosmic therapist knew that she could cure Betty's arthritis, but she also knew that the best time to begin her finger pressure treatments was at a time that Betty was not heavily afflicted by her painful malady.

It is at these moments that your patients are the most receptive to your healing power.

At an opportune moment, a moment when Betty was free of any remnant of her affliction, the treatments began. There has been no indication, up to the time of this writing, that Betty would suffer from arthritis in her right knee again. Betty has been free from pain during the six months that she has been undergoing Cosmic Finger Pressure Therapy. And there is no reason to believe that her illness will ever return again.

THE SEVEN WONDERS OF
COSMONOMIC FINGER PRESSURE

Finger pressure relies upon seven basic effects to stimulate the body to operate normally and to maintain balanced good health.

1. Stimulating the skin quickens the transportation of nourishment to the skin and helps to maintain a youthful appearance.

2. Stimulating the circulation of the body fluids reoxygenates the blood and aids in the blood's waste removal process.

3. Maintaining smooth muscle tone if one is to be free of stiff muscles and joints. Stiffness applies undue pressure upon the blood and nerve cells. This produces pain. Finger pressure therapy reduces tension and helps the muscles in stimulating the circulation of the blood and the correct functioning of the capillaries and nerve cells.

4. Making corrections to bone structure responds well to finger pressure. Cosmic therapy speeds up the nourishment that is required to keep the 206 bones of the human body healthy, balanced, and functioning in peak condition.

5. The nervous system controls all bodily actions and must be kept in perfect condition if illness, pain, and disease are to be erased from your life.

6. Cosmic Finger Pressure responsibly aids in activating the glands so that proper hormonal levels are maintained within the blood, and a proper chemical balance is maintained between the organs and the glands. Finger pressure helps to regulate the operation of the pituitary gland, as well as the testicles and the ovaries.

7. Stimulating the internal organs ensures that the organs function properly in oxygenating the blood and in removing waste products regularly and effectively.

HOW TO USE COSMIC FINGER
PRESSURE THERAPY EFFECTIVELY

Cosmic Finger Pressure activates certain psychic centers within your body. The psychic energy that is transmitted through your thumbs and fingers to these cosmic centers are impulses of health. These impulses are designed to ward off any illness or disease that might attack your body or the body of another.

As you read further into this chapter, I will give illustrated step-by-step instructions on how you can activate the various health centers of the body.

HOW TO BEGIN YOUR
COSMIC THERAPY

Before beginning your Finger Pressure Therapy, you should hold your arms against your sides, bending them upward at the elbow so that your fingers point toward the sky (as in the ritual you previously performed). When your fingers are pointing toward the sky repeat this simple affirmation of your cosmic power:

My fingers are filled with cosmic power, *Now!"*

Then, begin your treatment of the area or areas that your intuition leads you to. You do have an instinctive inner power that will influence you as to the correct area of the body to treat. The area where a future illness might show itself or where an affliction is already present will be instantly revealed to you. You will automatically reach for the correct psychic center to do your healing work upon.

HOW TO PERFORM THE COSMIC
FINGER PRESSURE THERAPY

After you have decided which energy centers to activate, place your finger or fingers on the cosmic spot as shown in Figure 1. Next, take a deep breath and say "Now!" You should then press the psychic center three times. *Push, Release. Push, Release. Push, Release.* Move on to the next center and repeat the therapy.

The pressure therapy depends upon the condition of yourself or your patient. It is just a matter of using your good common sense as to how hard you should press on these centers.

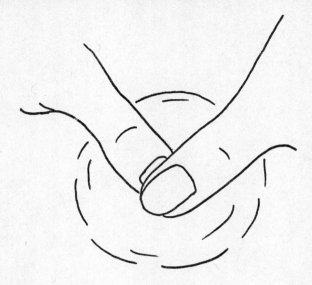

Figure 1

PERFORM YOUR COSMIC THERAPY WEEKLY

The obvious question is "How often should I perform my finger pressure therapy?"

The therapy is positive power. It should be applied one time each week or until the danger of contacting a disease has passed or the disease itself has been cured.

THE BODY'S ENERGY CENTERS ARE NUMEROUS BUT EASILY LOCATED

The energy cells that you are going to activate with your cosmic finger pressure are numerous. These centers are located in every part of the human body, with each energy cell controlling a certain area of the body—acting to keep that area in perfect health.

Figure 2 shows the frontal portion of the body, and the psychic centers that you will be performing cosmic therapy on.

There are also numerous energy centers that you will be working upon on the back side of the body (Figure 3).

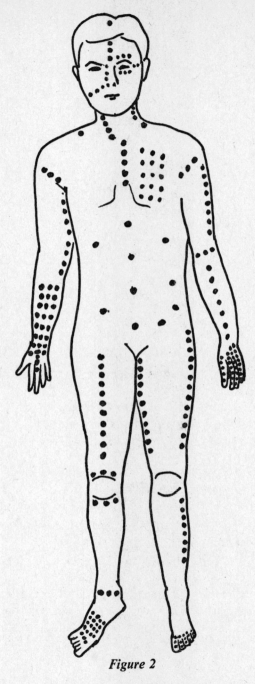

Figure 2

74

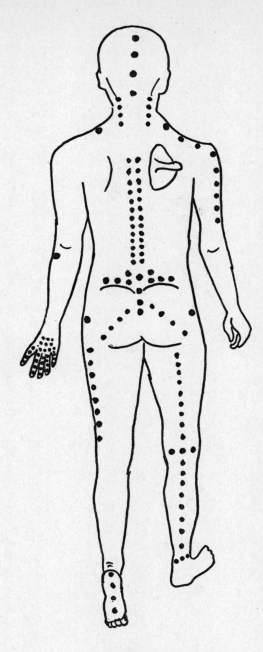

Figure 3

As this chapter progresses, I will give detailed instructions and visual illustrations that will make your Cosmic Finger Therapy a simple but effective tool in beating back pain and illness. Finger Pressure Therapy makes *you* the winner in the fight against disease, pain, or physical affliction.

COSMIC FINGER PRESSURE THERAPY
(TOP OF THE HEAD AREA)

Finger Pressure Therapy in the head area is said to cure common headache, migraine, insomnia, cerebral anemia, cerebral hyperemia, failing memory, senility, neuralgia within the nerve centers of the head, and balding (Figure 4).

Figure 4 reveals the psychic centers that you should activate to prevent or cure any of the illnesses described in the earlier paragraph.

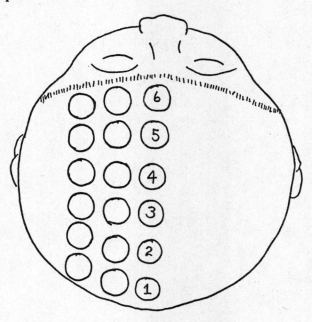

Figure 4

Begin your finger pressure at center 1 and work to center 6. When that has been completed, move to the left and follow the same procedure with the remaining twelve psychic centers.

These same nerve centers are also found on the right side of the top of the head. Activate these energy cells as soon as you have completed those at the left side of the head.

THE BACK OF THE NECK THERAPY

Figure 5 points out the seven points that must be activated to prevent insomnia, arteriosclerosis, migraine, neuralgia at the back of the head, hysteria, whiplash, and hangovers.

Remember! Your therapy begins with *Press, Release. Press Release. Press, Release.* This press and release should be done with rhythm—never with a jerking or nervous motion.

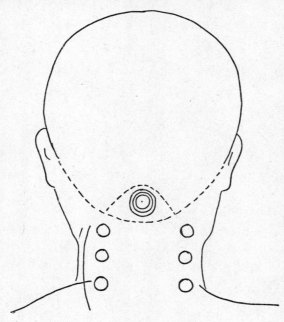

Figure 5

HOW TO PERFORM FINGER PRESSURE
THERAPY IN THE FACIAL AREA

The finger pressure exercises in the facial area are primarily designed to improve the facial appearance, e.g., the eyes, nose, and forehead. But in addition to the beautifying effects of the facial therapy, significant results have been noted for the prevention of tics, facial paralysis, nearsightedness, crossed eyes, and toothache.

With the same press and then release motion, perform your therapy upon the forehead at the psychic centers as shown in Figure 6.

When the exercises upon the forehead have been completed, move to the right and left sides of the face as shown in Figure 7.

This particular Cosmic Finger Pressure therapy has proven to be a favorite. It not only helps in preventing the aging process, but it leaves the face and facial muscles with a fresh new feeling as well.

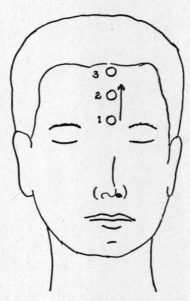

Figure 6

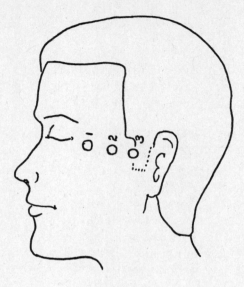

Figure 7

EACH PRESSURE POINT IS TO BE
PRESSED THREE TIMES

It often happens that the students of Medi-Cosmonomic Finger Pressure Therapy become overly zealous and skip rapidly from one pressure point to another. Finger therapy is not successful unless each psychic center is pressed upon three times in rhythm.

It takes little time to perform complete cosmic therapy—don't take shortcuts! Your therapy cannot be successful if you attempt to take a shorter route to perfection than this chapter indicates.

SIDE-OF-THE-NECK FINGER PRESSURE
IS VALUABLE THERAPY

If you sometimes sleep in unusual positions and greet the morning with a stiff neck, cosmic therapy can prevent this uncomfortable condition from arising again tomorrow morning. In addition to stiff muscles, this therapy is believed to prevent whiplash, dizziness, poor hearing, toothache, hangover, drowsiness, and motion sickness.

Begin this therapy at the top of the neck and work down toward the shoulder as shown in the diagram. Start at the front of the neck and work toward the back—press three times, release three times at each pressure point (Figure 8).

HOW TO CORRECT PROBLEMS OF THE FOOT, ANKLE, AND TOE

The most common complaints associated with these lower joints are arthritis, numbness, sprains, and gout. And Medi-Cosmonomic Finger Pressure can work wonders for these common inconveniences, but the cosmic fingers can accomplish much more than might be expected from therapy upon these areas.

Cosmic treatment upon the toes begins at the lower joints of the big toe. Three presses at that point, then three presses at the

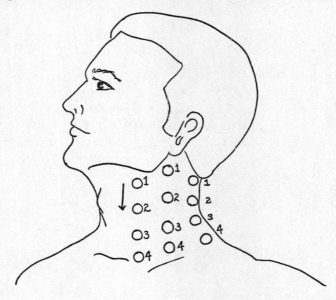

Figure 8

middle joint of the big toe, and finally, three presses at the top joint.

When cosmic energy has been pushed into those psychic centers, continue the same routine upon the other four toes before moving to the other foot (Figure 9).

Finger Pressure upon the instep regulates the functioning of the intestines. It prevents chills, headache, vertigo, numbness, gout, and cramps in the sole of the foot.

To perform cosmic pressure upon the instep, the therapist presses three times on the four sets of four points shown in Figure 10. Press all of the points 1, then points 2, 3, and 4 toward the ankle. Each point is pressed three times.

Points 1, 2, and 3 which are shown at the ankle are separate therapy. These cosmic energy centers prevent sprain and strengthen the ankle. Therapy in this area prevents and alleviates arthritis.

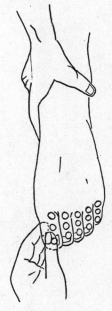

Figure 9

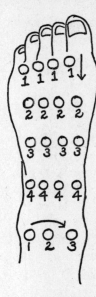

Figure 10

HOW TO USE COSMIC THERAPY PRESSURE
UPON THE FINGERS AND THE PALM

These treatments set up reactions that help regulate the healthful functioning of the internal organs and the brain. They prevent pain in the joints, numbness, gout, inflammation of the tendons, and pains in the heart.

The finger pressure should begin with the palm (Figure 11). Gentle pressure should be applied at points 1 and 3, but very heavy pressure should be applied at point 2. This pressure point (2), is one of the most important cosmic centers upon the body—it works to keep the heart young and active.

Finger pressure should begin just below the wrist as you introduce your cosmic energy to the pressure points upon the hand. When the psychic centers below the wrist have been energized, move to the area of the thumb and then to the area of the fingers.

There are many pressure points upon the hand that you will want to energize, but in using your therapy in a rhythmic fashion the entire hand can be covered in a very short time (Figure 12).

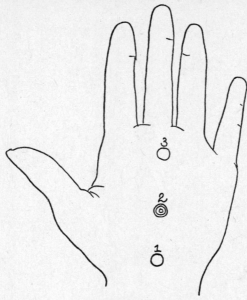

Figure 11

FINGER PRESSURE UPON THE
SIDES OF THE HEEL

Chills, burning sensations, cramps, and numbness in the feet can severly restrict the movements of an active person. And in addition, bed wetting, menstrual pains, irregularity, or kidney pains can incapacitate the average person.

Simple cosmic pressure upon the sides of the ankles can severely restrict the occurrence of these debilitating afflictions.

Follow the simple finger pressure illustrated in Figure 13 and prevent these inconvenient obstacles to healthy and happy living.

This same treatment should be continued upon the soles of the feet as further preventative or corrective medicine (Figure 14).

PREVENT PAINS IN THE HEART, PARALYSIS,
CRAMPS, GOUT, STRAINED MUSCLES, AND
WRITER'S CRAMP WITH FOREARM COSMIC THERAPY

There are twenty-seven pressure points on the under side of the forearm that must be cosmically activated and energized if you are to use this procedure as cosmic medicine (Figure 15).

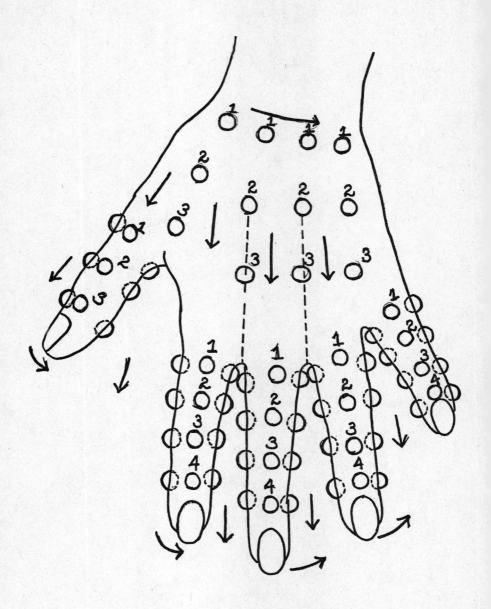

Figure 12

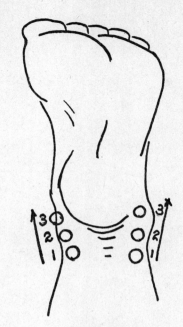

Figure 13

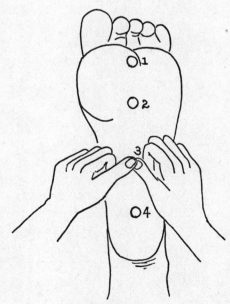

Figure 14

85

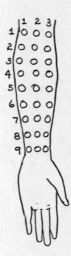

Figure 15

There are not shortcuts to Finger Pressure Therapy. Each cosmic point must be pressed upon three times. The soothing effect of this exercise will be a very pleasant surprise to the Cosmic Finger Pressure specialist as well as to the patient.

FINGER PRESSURE THERAPY AND THE ABDOMEN

Many physical irregularities are incipient within the abdominal cavity and it remains one of the most sensitive areas of the human body. Extra care should be taken that the pressure you apply to the energy centers is thorough, but very gentle in nature.

Common ailments and complaints that occur because of the poor regulation within this sensitive human cavity are loss of appetite, constipation, ulcers, stomach cramps, diabetes, liver trouble, menstrual irregularities, insomnia, neuralgia, irregularities of blood pressure, frigidity, poor digestion, gall stones, and kidney ailments.

This exercise in Cosmic Finger Pressure is essential to continuing good health. Use considerable good judgment in applying your finger pressure three times at each energy center. This portion of the body is a very sensitive and tender area to many people. Judge their overall physical condition before beginning the pressure therapy and proceed accordingly.

In this pressure therapy it is very important that you follow the instructions in the illustration exactly. Begin at point 1 and continue the pressure upon the centers in strict numerical sequence (Figure 16).

COSMIC FINGER PRESSURE
AND THE LEG

Three distinct areas at the back of the leg are vital for complete therapy in preventing or correcting cramps, swelling in the legs and joints, twists, sprains, fevers, and infertility in women.

The cosmic energy should first be applied just below the buttock, working your way to the three pressure points at the knee and continuing down the calf of the leg to the heel (Figure 17).

The cosmic therapy that you will perform on the back of the leg has such a relaxing effect that you, or your patient might drift gently off to sleep. This is nothing to be alarmed at; it is only a sign that your finger therapy is indeed effective and functioning in a well disciplined manner.

LET THE MIRACLE OF MEDI-COSMONOMIC POWER
BRING YOU SUCCESS, MONEY, HAPPINESS, LOVE,
POWER, AND PERFECT HEALTH, FOREVER

You have, undoubtedly, at this point in your Cosmonomic power program stepped back and exclaimed, "It's a miracle!" But your miracles have just begun.

You are now a healthy human being. And with your abundant good health and energy, now is not the time to stop and reflect upon your accomplishments nor to wonder how you performed your miracles.

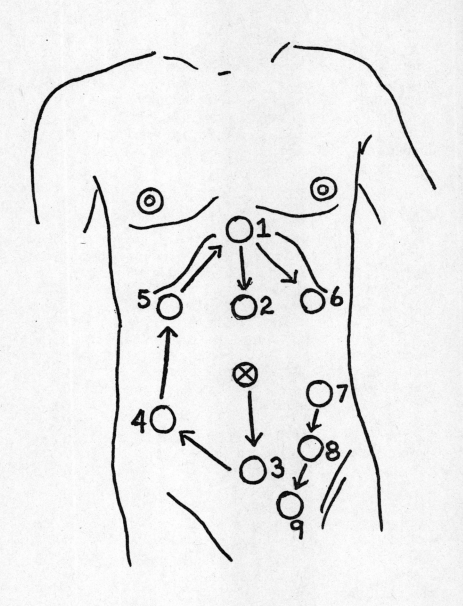

Figure 16

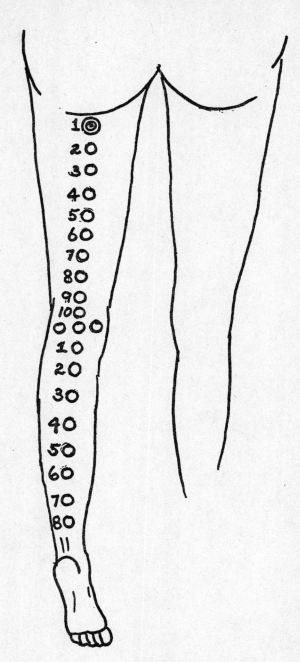

Figure 17

There are still dreams unfulfilled, but a healthy mind and body are necessary before there can be true enjoyment of your other pleasures of life. And it is in the next chapter that I will reveal even more secrets of Medi-Cosmonomic Medicine—the use of herbs and spices as an additional, healing psychic tool.

Chapter Four

HERBS, SPICES AND FOLKLORE: NATURE'S AMAZING UNIVERSAL MIND MEDICINE

In Chapter Three you learned the powerful secrets of healing as revealed through the miracles of Medi-Cosmonomic finger pressure. If you never learned another thing about the marvels of healing, the knowledge that you already possess marks you as a real "miracle worker." And yet, the Creative Mind that thrust the entire universe into being did not limit the methods by which we might restore our bodies to perfect health. Healing through the use of herbs is just one more psychic tool that is revealed to you in the pages of this powerful book.

YOU ALREADY ARE A PSYCHIC HEALER

Yes, you are already a psychic healer. And if you followed the instructions in Chapter Three, you are undoubtedly a very good one. Many Universal Mind students use both finger pressure and herbs in their healing efforts. Combining these two magical forms of healing produces miraculous results that can stagger the imagination.

ONE MAN'S WEED IS ANOTHER
MAN'S HERB

Oliver Wendell Holmes once defined a weed as any plant whose medicinal benefits have not yet been discovered. When the weed is found suitable as food or as a medicine, it is quickly elevated from its lowly position as a weed to the status of an herb.

Roving bands of Indians made a strong tea from the wild growing foxglove for those members of the tribe suffering from chest pains or heart trouble. Decades later medical science announced a new breakthrough in the treatment of certain heart ailments—digitalis! And from where was the new miracle drug extracted? From foxglove!

HOW GORDON L. AND VERN B. RESTORED
HAIR TO THEIR BALDING HEADS

Both Gordon and Vern are in their seventies, but "past forty" is how they describe their own ages. Both men have a full head of hair but swear that years ago they had "huge bald spots" on their heads. How did they restore hair to a bald spot? What wonder drug was it that made these men's hair begin to grow again? The same garlic that you find in the kitchen, your supermarket, or in your own garden.

Here are Gordon's instructions on how he and Vern covered their bald spots with a mane of hair.

Take a fresh clove of garlic, and cut a thin slice from the garlic clove three times a day. Rub the thinly sliced garlic into the bald spot. Between six and eight days, you'll see new hair sprouting in the bald spot. After the first sign of hair, continue the treatment for another three or four days.

It sounds too simple, doesn't it? It is simple, and because of the simplicity of herbal remedies most people pay for expensive drugs at the pharmacy, the same drugs that nature gives free-of-charge.

THE CATALYST THAT MAKES
THE HERB A MAGIC MEDICINE

Herbal medicine is effective, and it is powerful, but there is a catalyst that makes the herb the miracle medicine that it is meant to be. The activating agent, the essential ingredient that is required before the herb truly becomes a magic medicine is the psychic energy that I am going to teach you to produce.

In the past ages, it was the medicine man, the sage or seer that gave the herb the cosmonomic energy to perform its miraculous healing. And within the next few pages I am going to reveal the ritual that will give you the same power possessed by the ancient healer.

HOW HERBS CAN PROTECT THE
LUNGS OF CIGARETTE SMOKERS

Smoking is definitely not healthy for the human body and should be avoided, but if you are caught-up in the smoking habit you can protect yourself from possible future disease.

The Cosmonomic healer has been aware of Nature's "preventative medicine" for years, but it took the results of top researchers to give the herb its proper recognition.

Scientists in Pennsylvania and Lausanne, Switzerland announced that cysteine and ascorbic acid provided the body with protection against a chronic buildup of toxic gases arising from heavy smoking of cigarettes. These same scientists announced that these body protecting agents can be found naturally in barley, oatmeal, wheat gluten, peanuts, soybean, and sesame. Top biochemists have been gratified at the results of using cysteine and ascorbic acid to detoxify a harmful byproduct of smoking.

"WONDER DRUGS" ARE USUALLY
CULLED FROM ANCIENT FOLKLORE

In a previous paragraph I mentioned the wonder drug digitalis which is obtained from the dried leaves of foxglove. Digitalis is only one of the dozens of wonder drugs that have recently been "discovered" by science. But these same new wonder drugs have been used for centuries by the witch doctor, medicine man, saint, sage, and seer.

For the past few years, cortisone has played an active role within the medical field and has been prescribed to treat a variety of diseases and afflictions.

Cortisone in its natural and more effective state is found in wild yams and sarsaparilla.

Rutin is recognized within the medical field as an agent needed to insure healthy blood vessels and to prevent hemorrhage. And as thousands of people have discovered when they paid their bill at the pharmacy, it is an expensive synthesized medicine.

Rutin is derived from the very common rue, hydrangea, and forsythia.

Doctors have long been prescribing heparin as a medical agent to combat clots which lodge in the heart and lungs after coronaries. Heparin is a liver extract whose drawback is that it often makes patients ill.

The Mayo Clinic of Rochester, Minnesota, announced a new chemical found in yellow sweet clover. Not long after, two drug companies announced a new "wonder drug" that would "cure" coronaries. The New England Cosmonomic healer had known and used yellow sweet clover as a natural healing agent for generations.

The artificial wonder drugs that are prescribed by the physician to alleviate hardening of the arteries, which leads to the dreadful disease arteriosclerosis, are found in dandelions, spinach, and beet tops.

In reality, there have been no "new" wonder drugs discovered at all. The researcher has only given the scientific stamp-of-approval to medicines that have been known to the occulist for centuries.

HOW YOU CAN BECOME A
COSMONOMIC MEDICINE MAN

Herbs possess healing qualities for any person utilizing their ingredients, but their beneficial effects are limited until combined with your own Cosmonomic energy. It is your psychic energy that creates the environment in which the herb can work in complete harmony with every nerve and cell of the human body.

There is only one requirement that must be fulfilled before you begin the ritual that will allow you to join the growing society of Cosmonomic medicine men. The one requirement? Simply that you have an honest and sincere desire to not only keep your own body in perfect condition, but also a true humanitarian desire to ease the disease and afflictions of all mankind.

THE POWERFUL INITIATION RITUAL
INTO THE SOCIETY OF
COSMONOMIC MEDICINE MEN

There are no application forms, there are no dues, and there is not a role of membership kept as you join the society of Cosmonomic medicine men. Your ritual is performed in private, and your pledge is not made to man, but to the Creative Force of the universe.

Step 1. The ritual must be performed in the late evening and on the day of the week on which you were born. (If you were born on a Monday, perform your ritual on Monday. If you were born on Tuesday, perform your ritual on Tuesday, etc.) The ritual should begin upon the hour, e.g. 10:00 P.M., 11:00 P.M., midnight.

Step 2. Make absolutely certain that you are alone and will not be disturbed during the next few minutes.

Step 3. Kneel upon the floor facing east. (East is always symbolical of divine power.)

Step 4. Close your eyes and clasp your hands as if in prayer.

Step 5. With eyes still closed and hands clasped, tell the great Cosmic Consciousness why you want to become a Cosmonomic medicine man.
(If your motives be honorable, and your words heard by the Creative Force of nature, you will feel a slight tingling, or butterflies in the stomach.)

Step 6. Repeat this pledge aloud:

I,   (*name*)   , ask for admittance to the Secret Society of Cosmonomic Medicine Men.

I take this pledge with an open mind and an open heart. I will use my new powers only for Good. I will comfort the ill and diseased without prejudice or hope of material gain.

I acknowledge that there is no power but the power of Goodness and Mercy, and I now ask Thy benediction and blessing of divine approval. And so it is!

Step 7. Repeat this same ritual for the next three consecutive evenings and at exactly the same hour.

When Step 7 has been completed you will know that the hand of Providence has been placed upon you in blessing. You will feel differently. This will most probably be one of the most sacred and fulfilling experiences of your life.

WHAT IS AN HERB?

In today's usage, the accepted definition of an herb is, a soft succulent plant that is used for medicinal purposes, or for its sweet scent or flower.

In Cosmonomic language, the word herb means any vegetation that can be used for medicinal or cosmetic purposes.

Until two hundred years ago, the word herb was used to include fruits, vegetables, berries, the common spices such as mustard and salt, and was also used to include flavorings such as vinegar. The word vegetable was not even used in the English language prior to that time.

For purposes of this chapter, the word herb is used in its original sense as known two centuries ago. And as closely as possible, I will reveal the medicinal formulas of the herb as known to the alchemist, the witch doctor, the medicine man, and the occultist. Modern science has done little to improve upon the occult knowledge of the ancient seer or sage.

WHEN MODERN ANTIBIOTICS FAILED, THE DOCTOR TURNED TO PAPAYA FRUIT

You may have read of the remarkable recovery of Harris C. in a national magazine. Harris had undergone a kidney transplant and had developed a postoperative infection. Antibiotics failed to cure the infection. Harris was sinking quickly.

When Harris' condition appeared hopeless, a young doctor remembered that the natives in Africa had laid strips of papaya skin upon ulcerated wounds or infected areas. Without any regard to hygiene, the natives recovered.

Working quickly, the doctors placed strips of papaya over Harris' wound. In 48 hours, the infection had completely left the emaciated body. Harris returned to a full and active life.

Papaya is an unusual tropical fruit, and it is not always available in the supermarket. Harris' case history is given only to show that there are times that even the most advanced medical scientist must rely upon the herbal remedies revealed to you in this book.

DON'T IGNORE THE MEDICAL PROFESSION

All forms of healing are good! And once a person becomes ill, it makes little difference how the healing takes place.

Many people completely ignore the medical doctor, but this is a mistake. If you have a persistent ailment, by all means visit an M.D.

Former students who studied Medi-Cosmonomics have reported that they have discovered that there are many doctors who are quite willing to work with their patients who practice herbal medicine. One former student wrote, "My doctor was very interested in herbal medicine. He wrote no prescriptions and allowed me to gather my medicine from my own garden. He was both relieved and impressed that I had thrown away my sleeping pills and tranquilizers and replaced them with onions, lettuce, and celery."

DENNIS P.'S RHEUMATISM
WAS DIAGNOSED AS INCURABLE.
A CHANGE OF DIET LEFT HIM PAIN FREE.

Dennis P. is sixty-seven years old. For exercise, he literally pulls a car with his teeth.

It wasn't too long ago that Dennis was a hopeless cripple— almost unable to bear the pain from his swollen leg joints, wrists, and elbows. Dennis refused to accept the doctor's diagnosis of incurable disease and to retire to a rocking chair.

Dennis made a radical diet change. He gave up all red meats and replaced them with chicken and veal. He ate all of the green leafy vegetables he could hold and began a regular routine of light exercise. It took awhile, but Dennis is now completely pain free. He has the body of a forty-year old—and to prove his good health, Dennis really does pull a car with his teeth. Dennis' cure for rheumatism was so successful that he has now written a book on his amazing cure.

MOST MEDICINES PURCHASED FROM THE
DRUGSTORE CAN BE FOUND IN THE AVERAGE HOME

Americans are world famous for the number of pills they consume each year. Unknowingly, these unfortunate people are spending millions of dollars for medicine that can be found in the home—and at a very inexpensive cost. The dollars spent on unneeded drugs could buy many of the luxuries you may want for your home at this very moment.

Most prescription and over-the-counter drugs are for tonics, pain relievers, liver and kidney pills, tranquilizers and sleeping pills. The same ingredients found in these drugs are available to you in their natural form. Nature has given you an abundance of remedies to cure your every ill.

The table following lists herbs that can be taken to replace many of the drugs you may now be spending important dollars upon:

Drug	*Herbs*
Laxatives	Prunes
Iron Tonic	Spinach, Cabbage
Blood Purifier	Apples
Blood Tonics	Carrots, Cherries
Quinine	Dried Raspberries, Acid Fruits
General Tonics	Wild Cherries, Grapes
Liver Pills	Tomatoes
Aspirin	Radishes, Carrots, Turnips
Tranquilizers	Onions, Lettuce, Celery
Kidney Pills	Asparagus, Cauliflower

WASTE NOT, WANT NOT!

The four folklorian words of wisdom are important ingredients within your growing knowledge of Medi-Cosmonomic medicine. There are important uses for all parts of the herb—the tops from radishes, carrots and turnips contain the same medicine as the root. These herb tops are excellent as a steamed vegetable or added to soups, etc. The peel from the orange, tangerine, and lime are excellent when dried and grated and added to an herb tea, to jams, jellies, and preserves.

HOW MEDI-COSMONOMIC MEDICINE CURED MABLE T.'S HYPERTENSION

Mable T. had suffered from high blood pressure for years. "I was always a nervous wreck," she wrote. "I had become hyperactive, I talked too much, and just generally had a rotten disposition. I had very few friends left (I had insulted most of my friends to the point where they completely ignored me), and I was in danger of losing my husband.

"I really did follow the doctor's advice. I took my blood pressure pills and my tranquilizers exactly as prescribed, but nothing seemed to help.

"I had really become desperate," she continued. "I was sure that I was about to either have a nervous breakdown or suffer a stroke. It was at this time that I heard of Medi-Cosmonomic medicine. A friend suggested that I immediately begin eating as much fresh and uncooked onions, lettuce, celery, carrots, turnips, and radishes as I could. I was willing to try anything, but I honestly didn't expect any positive results. Was I ever in for a surprise!

"On the third day of my new diet I felt so calm and relaxed that I forgot to take my tranquilizers—I just didn't feel a need for them. Within a week I felt so very calm that I destroyed my entire supply of the tranquilizing drug.

"I was feeling so good, and was having such fun with my new and pleasing personality that I stopped my blood pressure medicine.

"I almost cancelled my next doctor's appointment, but I did want to see what Dr. J. had to say about my new condition. I was elated when he said that my blood pressure was completely normal. 'The medicine finally worked,' he said.

"He was amazed to hear that I had thrown my prescription medicine away and now relied entirely on nature's medicine.

"I've heard from others that Dr. J. now prescribes radishes, turnips, carrots, celery, lettuce, and onions for his patients suffering from hypertension. He now uses synthetic drugs only as a last resort."

HOW TO GIVE YOUR HERBS EVEN MORE MAGIC POWER

If you are growing your own herbs, it is very easy to give them increased energy and healing power.

Walk among your plants daily, and in a quiet frame-of-mind, point your fingers at the herbs, and as you do, declare this metaphysical truth:

You are filled with an abundance of Cosmonomic power, *now!*

You are filled with energy and now become nature's most magic healer.

If you are not able to grow your own magical herbs and must rely upon the supermarket, it is essential that you perform the same ritual as soon as you return home with your herbs.

First, place your herbs in the sink. Point your fingers at the vegetation and repeat the same declaration as if they were growing in your garden.

You are filled with an abundance of Cosmonomic power, *now!*

Your herbs are now ready to go to work—cleansing, soothing, and healing your body.

WHEN TO GATHER YOUR HERBS

All herbs should be gathered on the second of two successive days of sunshine. All herbs should be gathered before 10:00 A.M. if you are picking them fresh. The later the hour in the day, the less power or healing energy your herb will produce.

ADDITIONAL TIPS FOR HERB
GATHERING AND STORAGE

All herbs are best when fresh, but because of our growing seasons it becomes necessary to store some of your Ultra-Cosmonomic medicine.

1. Most herbs are ready to be cut just before blossoming.
2. Seeds are best collected as soon as they begin to ripen.

3. Never dry herbs with artificial heat.
4. Herbs dry best when hung in small bunches from the ceiling. There should be plenty of air circulation and the temperature about 70°.
5. Roots should be hung in cheesecloth or fine wire mesh. Turn or stir the roots daily.
6. Never crowd herbs or let them overlap. They will blacken and become useless.
7. Most herbs such as rosemary, thyme, etc., thrive the more you clip them. Let the herb grow to full height, and then keep it clipped back.

SCIENCE ANNOUNCES "NEW" POISON ANTIDOTE

This universal antidote for poisons whose origin is not known has been announced by Duke University. True, it is "new" to science, but an old remedy to the herbalist.

Universal Antidote:

Powdered burnt toast .... 2 parts
Milk of Magnesia .... 1 part
Strong Tea .... 1 part

Dose:

Two teaspoonsful in water.

With household poisoning becoming a very serious problem, the universal antidote given above is valuable knowledge for every Cosmonomic medicine man.

HELEN M.'S PSORIASIS WAS THOUGHT INCURABLE UNTIL SHE DISCOVERED SARSAPARILLA

Sarsaparilla is a native American root and grows abundantly in the wilds. Sarsaparilla is dried before use, so the root you buy at a health food store is as effective as one you roam the wilderness for.

A few decades ago sarsaparilla tea was a favorite drink as a tonic. There are few people who do not remember hearing their parents or grandparents expound the virtue of a good cup of sarsaparilla tea when one was tired or run down. Helen M. was one of these people who remembered grandpa sitting at the table with his cup of tea.

Helen had suffered from psoriasis for years. There were times she felt that the itching, flaking skin would drive her crazy—and she knew that there was no cure. She had her good days and her bad days, but was generally run down—not only from the constant need to scratch, but from the lack of sleep that ensued.

"When my skin became so blotchy with reddened sores that I was ashamed to go out in public," she told me, "I decided I just had to do something. My best girlfriend had offered to help me, but I didn't have any confidence in what I thought was mumbo-jumbo. My telephone call to her was the wisest thing I ever did."

Helen's friend Gladys had studied Medi-Cosmonomics and was one of the best Cosmonomic medicine men I had ever met.

Gladys went to Helen's house with a bag of sarsaparilla roots, and the rest is happy history.

"Gladys told me to grind up the roots and to drink four strong cups of sarsaparilla tea everyday. She also told me to mix the sarsaparilla powder into petroleum jelly and to rub it into those areas that were affecting me the most."

Helen continued. "I had suffered from psoriasis for years, but within two weeks, it left completely.

"I still feel the disease coming on occasionally, but before it hits me hard, I start drinking my tea. Within a day or two all signs of its appearance are gone."

MEDI-COSMONOMIC MEDICINE WORKS BEST WHEN YOUR BODY IS ON AN "UP" CYCLE

There is hardly a person that has not read or heard of the studies conducted on the "up" and "down" cycles of the human body. These body cycles are called biorhythms. Dozens of books have been written upon the subject, and if you have a desire to learn more about biorhythms than the information I give in this chapter, you can visit any library or bookstore.

The study of biorhythms really began in the fourth century B.C. when Hippocrates told his students to observe health fluctuations among well and ill people and to take these fluctuations into consideration when treating patients.

It has been found that your body undergoes a 23-day physical cycle that affects physical strength, endurance, energy, and resistance. At the high point of your physical cycle, you are best able to fight any illness that confronts you. At the low period of your cycle the opposite is true—you are susceptible to disease, and your body is less able to fight off negative influences that attempt to invade it.

At the high point of your physical cycle, Medi-Cosmonomics is best able to fight your illness with the help of your herbal knowledge and rituals.

It is at the low point of your physical cycle that you should use herbs, commonsense, and plenty of intuition to prevent your body from accepting a foreign intruder. Finding your own physical cycle with its "highs and lows" is a simple thing to do.

HOW TO DISCOVER THE HIGH AND
LOW DAYS OF YOUR PHYSICAL CYCLE

A few simple steps of elementary arithmetic will soon show you your good and your bad days, physically speaking. The first eleven days will show you your up cycle, the twelfth day is a neutral day, the following eleven days are your down cycle.

Follow these steps to establish your physical cycle:

1. Multiply your age by 365.
2. Add one day for each leap year.
3. Now add the number of days from your last birthday until today to Steps 1 and 2. You now have the total number of days that you've lived.
4. Divide the number of days you've lived by 23. This tells you the number of physical cycles you have lived. The remainder that is left from your division problem tells you how many days you are into your present physical cycle.

5. Take a calendar and mark your plus (+) and minus (−) days.

If, for example, your remainder is nine, you still have two plus days to go before you begin your down cycle. Mark the next two days on the calendar with + signs. Put a 0 that means neutral on the twelfth day and the following eleven days mark with a − sign, the following eleven with + signs, then a 0, then eleven minuses, etc. You can keep your physical cycle clearly marked on your calendar without ever again doing arithmetic calculations.

As your reputation as a Medi-Cosmonomic healer spreads, you will discover that determining the up and down physical cycles of your patients can have a strong influence upon your healing success.

HOW TO PREVENT OR SLOW DOWN
HARDENING OF THE ARTERIES

Arteriosclerosis is running a close second as America's number one killer. Commonly called hardening of the arteries, arteriosclerosis can be brought to a halt.

Cholesterol is the main villain and cause of this dreadful disease, but it can be avoided if you take a few simple precautions.

I do not mean to infer that every case of arteriosclerosis can be healed. Obviously, if you decide to eat all the meaty fat you can get your hands on, and your appetite becomes so large that you are very much overweight, nothing will help. But, if you maintain a normal weight and watch the fats that you eat, much can be done to prevent hardening of the arteries.

Cholesterol lines the walls of the coronary arteries and forces the heart to overwork. Two valuable substances have been found to lower the cholesterol content within the bloodstream—inositol and choline.

The names mean little to you, and you shouldn't make the effort to remember them. What is important, however, is that spinach, dandelions, and beet tops contain these substances, and it has been proven that these three herbs do help lower the cholesterol within the bloodstream.

HOW TO PREPARE SPINACH, DANDELIONS, AND BEET TOPS

The best results are obtained from these three important and powerful herbs when eaten raw. Mixing them into a green salad is a wonderful way to get your needed quantities of the herbs. If they must be cooked, they should be lightly steamed in as little water as possible.

FOLKLORE THAT CAN REMOVE THE TROUBLESOME WART

Mike R. was in his early twenties and had suffered from warts for as long as he could remember.

"They really didn't hurt," he said, "but I had so many warts that it was embarrassing. I had them on my hands and face as well as the rest of my body. I never took my clothes off to go swimming or to join in many of the sports other boys did. I was just too shy.

"I had tried all kinds of medicine—without success. The worst warts were removed by surgical means, but I had too many to ever hope that they could all be removed.

"One night I attended a talk you gave on Southern folklore. I was intrigued when I heard your remedy for warts. It sounded rather foolish, but I tried it anyway. I swear that it really worked!"

THE FOLKLORE RITUAL THAT WILL CURE COMMON WARTS

Tradition claims that this remedy first originated in Africa and was brought to America in the 1700's. At first, the folklore does sound foolish—just as Mike believed, but investigation will prove that the magic formula works as if by a miracle.

Any person who desires to remove warts need only follow these simple steps:

1. Find a bone upon which a dog has been chewing.
2. Pick up the bone with the right hand and touch it to the right shoulder exactly three times.
3. Rub the bone on any wart you desire to disappear.

4. When you have finished rubbing the warts take three steps forward and throw the bone over the left shoulder. *Do not look back at the bone!*

It's unbelievable, but warts will disappear overnight.

HOW LEONA M. THREW AWAY HER
DIET AND LOST FORTY POUNDS

This "diet recipe" is decades old, but it still remains one of the most effective diets discovered—and you can eat all that you want, but the only thing the dieter can eat is apples. It makes no difference whether the apples be green, red, or yellow. Eat all of them you can. Weigh yourself daily, and you will be amazed at the number of pounds that can be shed each day. This unusual occult diet can work the same marvelous results for you as it did for Leona. When you have reached your desired weight, resume your normal eating habits.

As a matter of added information on the apple, dentists have now discovered that the eating of an apple cleans the teeth better and prevents tooth decay and gum recession more effectively than brushing.

DON'T OVERLOOK THE IMPORTANCE OF YOUR
"DECLARATION" AS YOU MAKE YOUR HERBS READY FOR
USE

Herbal medicine will work without the power added to it by Medi-Cosmonomic declarations, but why use only half of nature's bountiful medicinal harvest when the knowledge given through Medi-Cosmonomics can give you the power to work miracles? Your rituals, in partnership with nature, provide you with the ultimate in Cosmonomic power. Don't overlook the Cosmonomic knowledge that has been revealed to you in previous paragraphs throughout this chapter.

HOW TO USE NATURE'S UNIVERSAL
COSMONOMIC MEDICINE

In a book of this size where the maximum effort is made to give you a broad and effective usage of all facets of Universal

Mind it would be impossible to cover the entire scope of Medi-Cosmonomic secrets. Due to this space limitation, I will direct my effort toward revealing the easiest found herbs that will cure the maximum number of illnesses.

Anise—Put the laxative back on the shelf. An herbal tea made with anise seeds guarantees results. As a cough remedy, place one teaspoon each of anise and thyme in a cup of boiling water. When cool, stir and strain. Add a teaspoon of honey. Sip two tablespoons every ½—1 hour.

Asparagus—Steam for three or four minutes. Asparagus contains large amounts of asparagine which is prescribed for kidney disorders. Asparagus is excellent for breaking up oxalic crystals in the kidneys and throughout the muscular system.
Asparagus is good in treating rheumatism, neuritis, etc.

Basil—Basil does not cure rheumatic pains, but it does temporarily allay rheumatic pain. In India, basil is considered to be a sacred plant. As a mild tonic for nervous disorders, basil, catnip, and peppermint prove to be a very effective tonic.

Preparation: Place 1/3 teaspoon of each herb in a cup of hot water for five minutes. Stir and strain. Sip slowly one such cup of tea 4—5 times a day.

Beets—Not only are vitamins A, B, C and G contained in the beet, but this wondrous herb also contains blood building minerals that are needed in the blood. The potassium content of the beet furnishes the general nourishment for all the physiological functions of the body.

Preparation: Best if grated and eaten uncooked. If cooked, steam for only a few minutes without removing the skins and eat the greens. They are an important article of food.

Blueberries—Besides being a tasty summer dessert, the leaves of the blueberry yield myrtillin, which is known to reduce the blood sugar as does insulin. The blueberry leaf has been used in the treatment of diabetes for many, many years.

Preparation: Steep a teaspoon of dried leaves in a cup of hot water. Drink one such cupful four times a day.

Cabbage—Roman physicians looked upon cabbage as a near cureall for headache, ulcers and insomnia. The modern Cosmonomic medicine man has discovered the ancient Romans to be correct.

The Stanford Medical School has discovered that fresh cabbage juice is an effective method of treating ulcers. It's good news for every Universal Mind student to read that a prestigious medical school has discovered what he or she already knew.

A glass of fresh cabbage juice can produce the same effect as a sleeping pill. There's no need to buy an expensive drug or to become addicted to a hard to break habit when nature's remedy for insomnia can be grown in a window box.

HOW RON R. CURED HIS MIGRAINE HEADACHES BY EATING CABBAGE

Millions of people suffer daily from migraine headaches. Though not a fatal illness, the pain and nausea caused by a migraine attack is unbelievably severe. Ron R. was one such migraine victim when he learned the wonders of the common cabbage.

"I am not exaggerating one bit when I say that I was about to 'end it all' when I met a Cosmonomic medicine man," Ron wrote. "I had suffered migraine attacks for twenty years and was very close to becoming a drug addict from the many pain killers I was taking daily. Seven days after I began eating raw cabbage, my headaches ceased. I haven't had a migraine attack in over two years!"

What Ron did was very simple. He kept a fresh head of cabbage handy. Any time that he felt like a snack, he would peel the leaves from the cabbage head and eat them.

It's very important that the cabbage be uncooked and uncut if it is to prove to be an effective medicine against the devastating effects of migraine.

Caraway, Peppermint and Spearmint—Nature's most effective antacid is a simple concoction of these three readily available ingredients.

Perform your magic ritual and add one-half teaspoon of each to a cup of hot water. Cover ten minutes. Stir and strain. Drink one cupful four times a day.

Carrot—The carrot is known as nature's protective food. Herbalists of the sixteenth century believed that "a carrot a day kept the doctor away." Notice that the ancient alchemist said a carrot—meaning one. One raw carrot a day is excellent Cosmonomic medicine, but eating several carrots each day does not give extra protection against disease—they will work in the opposite manner. Too many carrots a day can cause acute indigestion, and your skin will develop a distinctive yellowish hue.

Celery—Fresh and uncooked celery beats aspirin every time when it comes to combating the pain of nervous headache. If you have such a headache, eat a couple of stalks of celery. Your headache will quickly disappear.

Cherry—Either fresh or canned cherries can work wonders in the treatment of the common cold and arthritis. Sip cherry juice as a cold or cough remedy, and the eating of a dozen cherries a day has proven its power to give relief in cases of arthritis—cases of arthritis that have failed to respond to treatment by the professional medical practitioner.

I must admit that I let myself be carried away in my enthusiasm for the power of Medi-Cosmonomic medicine. It is difficult to limit my enthusiasm to the space allowed in this chapter, but there are so many Cosmonomic powers available to you that I must use discipline to keep this chapter to its proper length. For that reason, I will be brief in my explanations of the benefits of the remaining powerful Cosmonomic medicines.

Corn Silk—This easily stored Cosmonomic medicine is rich as an antibiotic and as an antihistamine in the treatment of certain allergies.

Dry the corn silk well and store in a can. Steep a teaspoon in a cup of hot water and let cool. Strain and drink four times a day.

Cranberry—This wonder medicine when drunk as a juice is excellent in the treatment of dysentery, scurvy, diarrhea, removes blood toxins, is effective in liver problems, checks fevers and asthma spasms.

Honey—The medicinal value of honey has been known for thousands of years. Nothing has been discovered as a more effective germ killer than honey. It produces miracles!

One man was burned from head to toe by scalding water. He came out of his ordeal with little pain and without a scar when honey packs were applied to his wounds.

HOW VERNAL A. USED LEMON PEEL
TO CLEAR HIS SKIN AND
LOOK TEN YEARS YOUNGER

Vernal A. had used every method he could find to cure his acne and blackheads. The expensive ointments prescribed by the dermatologist did nothing. A Cosmonomic medicine man suggested that Vernal rub his facial skin each night and morning with lemon peel. Vernal was quite surprised to note that this simple Medi-Cosmonomic formula did indeed clear his skin, but that wasn't all that it did.

Vernal told a group of friends who were kidding him about having had a "face lift" the simple truth.

"The only reason I used lemon peel on my skin was to clear up the acne, but there was an added side effect. The lemon peel actually tightened my skin!"

Everyone agreed that Vernal did indeed look ten years younger. Medi-Cosmonomics won many followers that day. Vernal's friends found that the simple lemon peel had the same effect upon their own sagging facial skin.

If you use this treatment upon yourself or others, you will soon discover that your magic ritual doubles the effectiveness of this wondrous Cosmonomic medicine.

Marigold—It has only been in recent years that the common marigold was planted in the garden as an ornamental flower.

At the beginning of the nineteenth century, the marigold was found only in the "herb or kitchen" garden.

Water distilled from the freshly picked flower head is an effective eye drop for red or sore eyes. When drunk, the marigold water promotes perspiration and is used in the treatment of measles.

Onion—I quote the miracle effects of the onion from a very old letter whose author remains unknown.

Onions, when plentifully eaten, produce sleep, help digestion, cure acid belchings, remove obstructions of the viscera, increase the urinary secretions, and promote insensible perspiration. Steeped all night in spring water, the infusion given children to drink in the morning while they are fasting kills worms. Onions burnished with the addition of a little fat and laid on fresh burns, draw out the fire and prevents them from blistering. Their use is fitted to cold weather and for aged, phlegmatic people whose lungs are stuffed and their breath short.

Potato—For burns, place thin slices of potato on the injured area. Remarkable healing will be on its way the very next day.

For skin diseases, eat one raw potato a day—the peel included. [To clean tarnished silver, soak in potato water for two hours.]

Radish—The radish was a popular medicine in ancient Greece and Rome. The early physician prescribed the eating of radishes each morning as the ideal "spring tonic." The Cosmonomic medicine man knows the miraculous benefits of the common radish.

Fresh radishes prevent gallstones and operate speedily to remove any gravel present within the system.

The drinking of a small amount of wine when eating the radish hastens the extraction of urine which effectively carries away poisons through the urinary tract.

Rose—The beautiful garden rose is nature's most prominent source of Vitamin C. The rose contains 60 times the amount of Vitamin C found in the lemon or orange. This bountiful supply of Vitamin C is found in the rose hip.

Boil the rose hip as you would any other fruit. When the cooking has been completed, strain, and cool. Drink one cupful of the rose hip water daily.

The rose plays an important role in the prevention of rupture and bleeding of the minute capillary vessels and aids in the healing of wounds.

Rosemary—This common, easily found herb can be used in a hundred different ways other than for its savory flavor in soups, salads, and main course dishes.

Mouth Wash: Steep one-third teaspoonful in one cup of water. Cool and strain.

Shampoo Rinse and Dandruff: Add one teaspoonful to a pint of hot water and let stand for 24 hours. Stir and add one teaspoonful of powdered borax.

Insect Repellant: Use equal parts of rosemary, lavender, and ground lemon peel. Crush together and apply to skin.

HERE'S TO YOUR NEW AND LONGER LIFE
OF GREATER HEALTH AND VITALITY

You have now learned more valuable secrets of Medi-Cosmonomics. In Chapter Three you discovered the miracle of Medi-Cosmonomic finger therapy, in this chapter, the miracle of the herb and the power of your own psychic energy.

There is no need to be ill. There is no need to look old when you can look years younger. There is no need to feel old or to act old when you have the secrets to restore vitality.

Yes, the miracle recipes that you learned in this chapter will work for people who do not believe in Cosmonomics—but they are only getting half a dose of nature's Cosmonomic medicine. It is only you, the Cosmonomic medicine man, who can bring the full force of healing power into your life and into the lives of those who have not had the good fortune to discover Medi-Cosmonomic secrets.

You now have health, vitality, and youth. What else could you possibly have need of? Well, how about money?

Turn the page to Chapter Five and learn how Universal Mind can bring you all of the money you can use.

DYNAMIC UNIVERSAL MIND RITUALS, CHANTS, AND AFFIRMATIONS TO BRING YOU ALL THE MONEY, LOVE, AND SUCCESS YOU CAN USE

The results of these rituals, chants, and affirmations will amaze you! Long before you finish reading this chapter, the Ultra-Cosmonomic Power will be filling your life with all of the money and love you can possibly handle.

CHANTS AND RITUALS ARE
MYSTIC COSMIC VIBRATIONS

The saints, sages, and seers of the ancient past discovered that certain chants and rituals created unique vibrations. These wizards of the ages also discovered that when they put certain vibrations into action, the pulsating vibrations sought like vibrations within the great Cosmic Mind. As these vibrations joined they became one pulsating force of energy that went to work to make a physical manifestation of its power. This physical manifestation was called a miracle. You will soon be creating the same miracles with the same powers experienced by the wise men of old. The Universal Mind Power is now waiting for you to put it into action. It wants you to experience health, wealth and happiness. It wants you to be a perfect human being. And, you soon will be!

MONEY HAS ALWAYS BEEN
A TROUBLEMAKER

Almost every person has trouble with money. There are a special few who inherit great wealth. They have trouble keeping the money that they've inherited and are constantly troubled in keeping their money from destroying their own ambition and will. They seek to lead a productive life based upon their own efforts.

The average person does not experience the same frustrations as those who are wealthy from birth, but, money, or the lack of it, is probably the most troublesome problem area in your life.

Money has always been troublesome, and for many people it probably always will be. You are going to have plenty of money before you finish this chapter, but money will not be a troublesome problem to you.

Cosmonomics is a system based upon working in harmony with the universe. Cosmonomics avoids conflicts until there is no other way to solve a problem or to create a miracle. If you understand what prosperity really is, money need not be the fearful, troublesome monster that many people make it out to be.

WHAT IS MONEY?

Money is really nothing more than pieces of printed paper or circles of metal. This paper and metal are just convenient symbols that you use to claim future goods and services. You entered life to become masters of life — not to be enslaved by life. You are intended to express more and more of life. You are meant to be rich, not poor. Cosmonomics will teach you to use its economic might. Cosmonomics will show you that you can multiply the symbols of wealth (money). Cosmonomics will show you that material prosperity is the highest of spiritual endeavors.

Many people believe that poverty leads to spirituality. This myth was perpetuated in the Middle Ages upon the slave and the serf. "Be content in your lowly station of life," the rich would say, "for yours is the kingdom of heaven," thus keeping the poor in a passive state of existence at the poverty level.

You are meant to experience life in material abundance. If you hold any doubts that you are meant to be rich, this chapter is not for you.

It is time to understand the truth. The love of money is a good emotion? It is a good emotion because you should have enough to fill every material need.

Greed is the negative emotion toward money. To hoard money in fear of not having enough is a negative affirmation that begs for poverty.

Forget any fear of poverty that you might hold.

Do not hoard money from fear of lack.

Accept the fact that you will always experience material abundance.

You have now discovered the essence of the Principle of Cosmonomic Abundance.

YOUR FIRST STEP UPON THE PATH
TO COSMONOMIC PROSPERITY

Hopefully you have overcome any doubts that you might have harbored that abundance is not spiritually wholesome.

The first step to an abundance is acceptance of a fact-of-life. We live in an economic, materially oriented society. Riches must lead to ever increasing effectiveness, and the logical first step is good health.

Without good health you can neither be effective nor can you truly enjoy your new found wealth. This chapter, as well as Chapters Two and Four, presents you with alternative solutions to any health problem. Use your Medi-Cosmonomic knowledge to reach a state of perfect health. When you have, you are ready to take another step forward on your path to material wealth that will leave your friends and family awestruck as you become more prosperous with each passing day.

COSMONOMIC PROSPERITY'S SECOND STEP

Enthusiasm and good sportsmanship are step two of Cosmonomics' road to ever increasing abundance.

If you do not possess a positive attitude toward life you can little enjoy the prosperity that is about to become yours.

Life is an endless series of games, and if you are to succeed in these games of life you must have enthusiasm — the will to win.

And as you play these games of life you must develop a healthy sense of good sportsmanship — play life by the rules. There would be little satisfaction experienced if you were to win a game by cheating. What profit would there be if you were to lose the respect of friends and family by relying upon unethical or immoral means to achieve prosperity? Wealth would soon become a burden rather than a blessing.

If you want to be rich, play by the rules!

THE COSMONOMIC PROSPERITY CURRENT

A current of prosperity is enveloping you at this very moment. You may not feel the waves of prosperity power that now surround you, but they are there, and they always have been — since the moment of your birth.

Your Cosmonomic step three is to wipe all negative influences and thoughts of poverty from your mind. You must simply be willing to accept the fact that for the rest of your life you will experience nothing but material abundance.

Believe it or not, many people find it difficult to accept the fact that they are about to receive an abundance of material wealth. Don't let yourself be one of the unfortunate people that believe that lack and poverty are an inevitable part of living in a material world, for they are not!

PROSPERITY!
STEP FOUR

You're now ready to accept the prosperity that was your birthright. The Cosmonomic step four will push the button to unleash a flood of prosperity into your life.

Each morning and evening, you must devote at least five minutes to performing any of the chants, rituals, or affirmations that you will find in this chapter. They all work, and one is as effective as the other. Just find the ritual, chant, or affirmation that feels to be the best suited to your own personality and begin your new and adventurous life as a financially carefree individual.

HOW YOU CAN QUICKLY LOSE ALL
OF YOUR FINANCIAL GAINS

The quickest road to poverty and grief is selfishness and greed. There is no need to hoard your material gains — there's plenty more where that came from. If you store up for fear of lack, it is lack that you will harvest.

The magic key that keeps abundance flowing into your life is your willingness to give of what you have received. The giving can take many forms, but give you must.

This spring, my wife, our friend Dave Early and I mailed over 1500 iris flower plants to senior citizens, veteran's hospitals, and other recipients in 48 of the 50 States. We cared little about the material value of our gifts and had no doubts that the $3,000 we were giving away would soon be replaced, and it was! Within days of the mailing of our first package the three of us met with an almost unbelievable string of good luck. The money spent just primed the material pump. New avenues of prosperity opened up to us so quickly that we were barely able to handle them.

WHEN ARTHUR F. AGREED TO UNSELFISHLY GIVE AWAY MONEY HE COULD NOT AFFORD, A COSMONOMIC MIRACLE OCCURRED

Arthur F.'s parents were being forced to move when the owner sold the apartment they were renting. Try as they might, Mr. and Mrs. F. could not find another place to move that they could afford on their limited pension.

Arthur knew the kind of home his parents wanted — a duplex with a small yard and all the modern conveniences, and in the best part of town. He quickly found the ideal duplex, but the rent was far more than his parents could afford. Arthur talked to the landlord and made a confidential agreement to pay the difference in the rent, unknown to his parents.

At the moment Arthur signed the agreement, he did not have the extra $100 a month he would be paying, but he had every confidence that he had done the right thing and that he would have the extra money required.

It was one week after Arthur had signed the secret agreement that his boss called him into the office. "I just wanted to tell you that beginning today, your salary is being increased by $150 a month." Arthur had experienced previous Cosmonomic prosperity miracles, but he couldn't hide the big smile as he walked from the boss' office. If your motives are right, you too will experience miracles just as Arthur did.

ADJUST SHORT TERM APPEARANCES FOR LONG TERM GOALS

When Dan E. developed a product that would make life more enjoyable it appeared that he was poor. It looked highly unlikely that he could ever get the product on the market. His total savings were $100.

Dan went into debt as he purchased enough material on credit from his potential suppliers to produce a few samples of his product. He used his $100 to advertise what he had to sell. He sold enough on the first go-around to have $300. He spent this entire amount on more advertising, never doubting for a moment that his present indebtedness was only a short term inconvenience. His vision saw only his long term goal — wealth. Dan's business pyramided, and within three years he sold his company for several million dollars.

If you want to experience the same success as Dan, don't let negative thinking interfere with your long-term goals. There are times, as in Dan's case, when indebtedness is an essential ingredient before wealth and luxury can be obtained. As in all matters of this kind, it is you that must use good, sound, judgment in your business affairs.

LET MONEY DO MORE THAN BUY MATERIAL POSSESSIONS

At the beginning of this chapter I wrote that money is only a "symbol that you use to claim future goods and services." That phrase remains true, but let's expand your consciousness a bit when we speak of money.

There are many rich people who are absolutely miserable. They have every material possession that money can buy. Obviously, money has not resolved their troubles or their woes. These super-rich have not discovered that money can buy more for them than material possessions. Make sure that you don't develop this same "tunnel vision" as your own riches increase.

What else can money buy? Many things, e.g., security, education, and peace of mind.

Money should give you mental and emotional security — no more fear of lack, fear of poverty, bill collectors at the door. Cosmonomic prosperity leaves you with a feeling of security in the world. Your mind is cleansed of fear and negative thinking. Your mind is free to accept the truly beautiful world in which you live.

Money can give you the opportunity for education, the opportunity to expand your mind to its limit. I do not necessarily refer to a formal college education — though that is readily available. I refer to the money available to buy books, the opportunity to travel, the opportunity to attend all of the cultural activities your heart desires, and a hundred other ways that money can expand your heart and your mind.

And what about peace-of-mind? Can you really be happy without peace-of-mind? As you have probably discovered in the past for yourself, the answer is an empathic, *no*! A dollar value cannot be placed upon peace-of-mind, but what is life without it — drab and filled with conflict, at best.

Now that you've realized the tremendous potential for greatness that money can bring into your life, open the floodgate to unlimited riches and bask in the flow of financial security that will remain with your forever.

THE POWERFUL PROSPERITY RITUAL
THAT GIVES YOU THE KING MIDAS GOLDEN TOUCH

This powerful ritual is so simple that many people doubt that it will work — but they soon discover that it really does work. And it takes such little effort.

This ritual I consider to be a general purpose prosperity formula. It won't bring you any extra money that you will have to worry about; it simply brings you the amount of prosperity that you actually need at any specific moment. Besides money, it will bring you success, health, love, security. The ritual brings you just what you have need of. It brings you a perfect miracle at the exact moment you need it. Your link to the great creative power of Universal Mind is unique and individualized. The miracle is designed for your benefit only.

Step 1: Choose a person or an organization that you feel is worthy of a material donation or reward.

Step 2: Find some type of vessel in which you can store quarters (a tin can, cup, glass, vase or bottle are all suitable containers for your twenty-five cent pieces).

Step 3: When you have found a suitable container, clutch it in your hands and repeat these words:

Thou are now a sacred vessel — a vessel filled with eternal power and prosperity. Thou shalt weave the web of material abundance throughout the universe and draw my riches to me. And so it is!

Step 4: Each night before retiring, hold a quarter in the palm of your left hand and repeat this affirmation:

I dip my hand into the well-spring of prosperity, and my cup runneth over.

When the affirmation has been completed, drop the quarter into your sacred vessel.

Step 5: Once each month, empty the contents from your sacred vessel and send the contents to the person or organization you wish to honor with your donation.

Sound simple? It really is simple for you, and it really does work; but, unseen to you, powerful cosmic forces are at work to make even your most complex desire become a reality. Your tithe or donation is the key to positive future riches.

Here is a true case history of what happened to Marvin L. when he began his twenty-five cent a day cosmic investment.

HOW MARVIN L. WENT FROM COMMON LABORER TO CONSTRUCTION FOREMAN

Marvin L. was a common construction laborer in America's fastest growing county (Santa Clara County, California). Marvin had been a laborer for years and held little hope for any relief from his back-breaking labors. Because of stiff union rules, there was even smaller hope of being accepted into one of the more skilled and higher paying trades.

Marvin had done everything he could to advance himself in the material world — everything except use the Cosmonomic Prosperity Formula.

Marv's wife had become interested in Universal Mind power as the result of a personal healing she had received from a Cosmonomic finger pressure therapist. It was at her insistence that Marvin began his nightly affirmation ritual. This is how Marvin explained to me his sudden rise from laborer to construction foreman.

Before I began my 25 cent-a-day cosmic investment, I had no confidence at all that it would work. As a matter-of-fact, I thought I'd be giving much needed money away to an organization that probably needed the money less than I did, but a strange feeling came over me the first night that I performed the Ritual of the Sacred Vessel.

I had just finished the ritual, and a sudden warm, tingling sensation seemed to throb throughout my entire body. I felt renewed. I felt reborn. But mostly I felt confidence. I was confident that I was going to succeed. I knew that I was going to become prosperous. I was so sure of it that not once did I feel doubt or negativity within myself.

Things went along as normal for the first few days after I had begun my prosperity ritual, but after a couple of weeks, the owner of the construction firm began to drop by the construction site with almost daily regularity. It wasn't too long before we became fast friends.

It was just about five weeks after I had begun my prosperity ritual that Mr. J. told me that he was going to begin a new housing development in the foothills of the Sierra Mountains. "Would you consider accepting the job of foreman?" he asked. Of course I said, "Yes."

I have never been happier. We have all the money we want. I have a job that makes me very happy. There is nothing more that I could ask for. Thanks to the Universal Mind for giving me what I consider to be a perfect life.

THE MYSTIC CHANT THAT
WILL WIN CONTESTS

A chant is an affirmation, prayer or command that is spoken to a particular rhythm. The occultist knows that the vibration sent into the universe at a certain pulsating rythm seeks out its own. As the two forces meet and connect, tremendous power is generated. This powerful cosmonomic force returns in all of its cosmic splendor and creates a miracle. The chant that I am about to reveal to you must be spoken aloud in a sing-song, up-and-down manner.

Before you begin saying the chant, practice aloud by counting from one to seven in the same sing-song fashion that you will use when using your chant to win a contest. As you practice one, two, three, four, five, six, seven, you will notice that you are developing a very definite rhythm as you pronounce the numbers. This same rhythm should be used as you use the mystic chant to win contests.

In metaphysics, the number one is symbolical of creation, the number seven is symbolical of completion. The magical chant that you will be using is written in this metaphysical manner. Line one has one word, line two, two words. Line three has three rhythmic beats, etc. The chant ends with a line that has seven beats. This symbolizes success, completion. It is the cosmic manifestation that makes you a winner.

NOW
I SPEAK
TO COSMIC MIND.
I CO-MAND THAT
THE IN-FIN-ITE POWER
OF GOOD AND RIGHT O-BEY
MY HEART'S DE-SIRE. I PROSPER NOW!

You can make your own metaphysical cosmonomic chant pyramid by following very simple rules.

Line one must have one rhythmic beat, line two, two beats, etc. You can use this powerful word pyramid to create a chant to fulfill every one of your desires. These cosmonomic pyramids do work miracles.

HOW MARIANNE K. WON
A NEW AUTOMOBILE TWO YEARS
IN A ROW AT THE CHURCH BAZAAR

This true case history happened several years ago in Denver, Colorado. I have newer case histories to prove the power of the mystic chant to win contests, but this case history of Marianne K. has remained one of my favorites.

Marianne K. worked very hard at her church's yearly bazaar. The bazaar helped to raise money that was used to subsidize the private school that was operated by the church.

Marianne bought $1.00 chances on several items to be given away at each bazaar. She never expected to win, and she didn't. She looked upon her numerous $1.00 ticket purchases simply as donations.

After a year of bad luck, Marianne changed her thinking from I don't expect to win, to I do expect to win. I need to win! Her automobile was ready for the scrap heap, and she needed to win the new auto that would be given away at the last drawing of the church bazaar.

Marianne made up her own mystic chant to win contests and she did win. She won a brand new auto on a one-dollar chance.

Marianne was elated with her new auto and she had only driven it 5,000 miles when next years' bazaar approached.

"It was really more for fun than anything else that I performed my mystic ritual at the bazaar the year after I had won my auto.

"I bought a one-dollar chance on the drawing for the auto that year, and believe it or not, my name was drawn as the winner of a new auto for the second year in a row. I was really sorry that I had won. There were a lot of people who swore the drawing was crooked, but it most certainly was not. Anyone who really needed the car could have performed his own mystic chant and won, if he wanted to and needed the car worse than I did."

A professor at the univesity calculated that the chances of Marianne's ticket being drawn two years in a row were over 300 million to one.

Marianne's story is positive proof of the ultra-power of Universal Mind.

A SECOND POWERFUL AFFIRMATION
THAT BRINGS YOU MONEY AND SUCCESS

Great truths and powerful secrets often appear simple, and usually they are simple. Most people are failures because they erroneously believe that miracles can only be achieved by complex formulas, complex rituals, fasting, or whatever. Their very efforts to make a simple truth complex slams the door on any blessing that might have come their way.

A chance acquaintance that I made at a charity fund raising dinner shared his secret of prosperity with me over the banquet table. He obviously had had a very enlightened prosperity teacher.

I am sorry that I cannot recall the teacher's name so that I might give her the proper recognition within these paragraphs. But as all enlightened teachers, I am convinced that she would much prefer the recognition of cosmic truth, rather than the recognition of her individual personality.

The gentleman at the banquet, as I recall, told me of a group of business people who were meeting weekly to experiment with prosperity affirmations during a deep business recession.

Each week the class wrote down their prosperity desires. During the week they changed, revised and expanded their lists as circumstances dictated. No one saw the lists other than the individual business person making the list. Within two months, every person attending the experimental prosperity workshop had achieved his goals — and here is how you can do the very same thing.

Step 1: Make a list of definite things that you want or the amount of money you want to receive.

Step 2: Remove all negative thinking from your thoughts. Imagine that you're like the farmer. He plants the seed in the spring, and he has no doubts that he will have a bountiful harvest in the fall. You are planting prosperity seeds. Expect a bountiful harvest.

Step 3: Update, revise or change your prosperity list on a daily basis.

Step 4: Repeat the powerful prosperity formula that follows at least once each day. Even better, repeat it as often as possible throughout your busy day.

I am the rich and majestic child of Universal Mind. All that the universe has is mine to share and experience for myself.

The Great Universal Mind is now showing me how to obtain my own freely given wealth. Every door opens wide to give me my immediate rewards. I have confidence that all that is mine will come to me in rich abundance from the great creative force of all prosperity. My riches do not interfere with anyone else's good, since Cosmonomic riches are unlimited and everywhere for all to use. That which is not for my good fades from me, and I no longer desire it, or accept it. The great riches of the Cosmonomic source of all good now floods my life with riches and material abundance. I accept no other way.

HOW THIS AUTHOR USED AFFIRMATIONS
TO WRITE PSYCHIC TELEMETRY[1]

During 1975, my subconscious mind kept nudging me to write a book covering some of the lessons I had learned during my two decades as an occult-psychic teacher. I had been successful in magazine writing, but I really doubted that I wanted to develop the self-discipline necessary to write a 65,000 word book. Grudgingly I gave into my subconscious cosmic mind and sat down to write a couple of sample chapters. I then began to mentally broadcast affirmations to lead me to the right publisher and finally to the right editor at the publishing firm.

After a few days, there was no doubt but that I should submit my sample work to Parker Publishing. The manuscript was mailed with the positive affirmation that the right editor at Parker receive my work. The affirmations paid huge dividends. Before long I received my contract from Parker.

My editor suggested various approaches that I might take in realizing my goal of writing a unique psychic-occult book. My affirmations continued, and it became more and more obvious that Universal Mind had certainly had a hand in selecting my editor.

I began writing *Psychic Telemetry* in June, all the while using affirmations that Universal Mind would express through me 65,000 words of valuable psychic information. I wrote on Saturdays only, continually using affirmations and psychic commands to help me in my endeavors.

---

[1] *Op. cit.*, p. 66.

Psychic Telemetry began in June and was completed by September. In October the manuscript was returned, the editor asking me to rewrite two paragraphs of the Introduction. Now that's not bad! A novice author rewriting only two paragraphs out of 65,000 words is very unusual indeed. A miracle? I know it was!

I'm telling you of this personal case history only to prove the efficiency and reliability of affirmations. I'm not telling you the story to build my own ego, for I am quite aware that I personally had little to do in developing what I believe was a very worthwhile book.

As a matter-of-fact, I'm using affirmations to write the book you are reading at this very moment. As I make ready to begin a new chapter I simply say:

I now write a chapter on _____ _____ _____
_____. Fill my mind with cosmic knowledge *now*! And so it is!

THE COSMONOMIC RITUAL
THAT BRINGS SUCCESS EVERY TIME

There are hundreds of reasons why success is not achieved by thousands of talented and qualified people, but the greatest obstacle to success is (as I continually repeat), lack of confidence which leads to negative thinking. Negative thinking leads to imprisonment of the mind. Once imprisoned, there is little room left to strive for success.

You know people this very moment who are successful and you wonder why when there are dozens of people more qualified that are failures. There is no secret as to how success is reached. Goethe expressed the answer very well:

What you can do or dream you can, begin it.
Boldness has genius, power and magic in it.

With the help of Universal Mind, whatever within your mind you can conceive, you can achieve!

The entire universe is a mass of pulsating vibrations. These vibrations blend, mix, cross, and infiltrate each other. Because of these crosscurrent vibrations, various types of vibrations pulsate more strongly from one direction than another. In the desire for success or material prosperity, the direction from which the greatest cosmic material power flows is from the north.

HOW TO PERFORM THE
COSMONOMIC SUCCESS RITUAL

Your first step toward achieving new success is to decide what you want to be successful doing. Success will be very allusive if you don't know what you want to claim your success from.

To perform the powerful ritual you must be out-of-doors, and preferably out-of-sight from curious onlookers (a quiet park, the beach, or the mountains are ideal retreats).

When you have found your own secluded area in which to perform your ritual, face due north, grasping ten pennies in your right hand. You are now going to take ten steps forward. With each step you are to take one penny from your right hand with your left hand. As you take a step forward, throw the penny from your left hand over your right shoulder. Do not look back! With each step forward you will also repeat an affirmation. Now follow my instructions exactly as you perform this ritual.

1. Face directly north, holding ten pennies in your *right* hand.
2. Take one step forward with your *left* foot.
3. Bring your *right* foot forward, to rest next to your left foot.
4. Take one penny from your right hand and hold it in your left hand.
5. Throw the penny in your left hand over your right shoulder.
6. Repeat this affirmation:
   I am successful in all that I do and say.

Continue with your next step forward and throw another penny over your right shoulder. There is, however, a different affirmation that you are to say as you take ten magic steps to success.

At your second step repeat this affirmation:

I am sucecssful in all that I think and feel

At your third step, repeat:

I am successful in all that I hear and see.

At the fourth step:

I am successful in reaching my stated goal (express your desire).

And at the fifth step, repeat:

I am successful in love and happiness.

After the sixth step:

I am successful in all of my material endeavors.

After the seventh step, repeat:

I am successful in becoming attractive to all people who might bring benefit into my life.

When you have taken your eighth step and thrown the penny over your shoulder, continue with your affirmations.

I am successful in bringing healing and perfect health to myself.

After your ninth step repeat this very important affirmation:

I am successful in removing all doubts, despair, and bitterness from my mind and my heart.

At your tenth step, repeat:

My success is now assured. No power can keep me from the success that is divinely mine. I am a perfect creature living in a perfect universe.

HOW TO END YOUR
MYSTIC RITUAL

After you have completed your ten steps to the north and have said your affirmations, turn and face the east. It is from the east that eternal wisdom flows.

With head slightly bowed, speak your owns words of

thanksgiving to the Universal Mind. Have no doubts. You will be successful.

PROGRAM YOUR SUBCONSCIOUS MIND
TO WORK FOR YOU 24 HOURS A DAY

In this active, busy world, it is sometimes difficult to find a peaceful time in which to perform your chants, rituals, or affirmations. Luckily for mankind, the Creative Force that knows all things realizes that we are sometimes burdened by daily pressures and cannot clear our minds of the material details that need our immediate attention. The Ultra-Cosmonomic Mind gave you a way to solve this dilemma. Our ultra-powerful minds can be put to use while our conscious mind is at rest or asleep.

HOW TO PROGRAM YOUR SUBCONSCIOUS
MIND TO WORK FOR YOU WHILE YOU
PEACEFULLY SLEEP AWAY THE HOURS

Just as you go to bed, darken the room and lie flat upon your back with your hands at your sides. Do not use a pillow, as the bend or kink in your neck will interfere with the flow of psychic energy that will be created within your abdomen. This psychic energy must flow directly and without restriction to your own subconscious mind.

You are now comfortable. Clear your mind of the troubles of the day and visualize what miracle you now want to manifest within your life. When the desired miracle is fully visualized, say this positive psychic command:

I now command that my subconscious mind be responsive to my wants, my needs, and my desires. Whether I be awake, or asleep, the Ultra Cosmonomic Power works every hour and every minute to fulfill my every wish. I do not doubt. I do not question. My miracle will appear at the proper moment and in accordance with the perfect methods of the Cosmonomic Creative Power. And so it is!

HOW ETHYL B. USED A CHANT
TO FRIGHTEN HER ATTACKER AWAY

Ethyl B. was walking from the supermarket to her auto when a man jumped from behind the parked cars. He grabbed for

Ethyl's purse. Ethyl resisted and was knocked to the ground. Ethyl kept her wits. While still on the ground she began her mystic chant.

As Ethyl chanted, her would be attacker stood as if paralyzed. Fear hung heavily upon his face. At the last word of Ethyl's chant the attacker screamed and ran wildly through the parking lot.

Ethyl received a slight bruise, but without her mystic chant for self-protection, her injuries would certainly have been more serious. And, the thief did not succeed in his efforts to steal Ethyl's handbag.

THE MYSTIC CHANT WORKS
ONLY AGAINST EVIL

Quite frankly, this chant works as a curse upon any person that would do you physical harm. You need not be concerned that you are committing an evil deed by pronouncing a curse. Nor should you be concerned that you might place a curse upon an innocent person.

Cosmonomics works only good. It is fair to all people, and this Universal Power does indeed play by the rules.

This chant will only work against the person intending to do you any form of physical harm. If the chant is pronounced against an innocent person, it will not work. The chant is completely ineffective unless it is used against evil. It will never work against good.

THE MYSTIC CHANT FOR
SELF-PROTECTION

Unlike the previous chant that was to be said with a sing-song effect, this chant should be expressed in a low, smooth, monotone voice.

I
PLACE A
CURSE U - PON
YOUR HEAD. THE GATES
OF HELL HAVE O - PENED
WIDE. MIS - ERY AND SUFFER - ING
WILL FOLL - OW THRU E - TERN - ITY.

HOW TO WIN FRIENDS AND
INFLUENCE PEOPLE

The secret chant I will soon reveal to you will win all the friends you can possibly want. The Cosmonomic power of the chant will influence people who are hundreds or even thousands of miles away. But in winning friends or influencing people you must accept certain responsibilities that inevitably follow. Most of these responsibilities are revealed through your own common sense.

This secret chant will win all of the friendships you desire, but it's up to you to keep the friendships once they appear in your life. If you want to keep friends, you must learn to be a friend.

It's a very simple thing to influence the thoughts of others, but don't do it just for practice or to gain a personal satisfaction as you watch others move to the commands of your secret thoughts.

THE SECRET CHANT THAT
WILL WIN ALL OF THE FRIENDSHIPS
YOU CAN POSSIBLY DESIRE

This chant is so effective that it should be used with caution. Many people have used this chant to discover that they have so many new friends that they just do not have enough time in the day to devote to keeping so many friendships active and alive. Ill will can be created as you are forced to become selective and limit the number of friendships that can be easily and profitably enjoyed.

I
AM A
FRIEND TO ALL,
AND ALL A FRIEND
TO ME. THOSE BRING - ING
JOY TO MY LIFE ARE NOW
DRAWN TO ME AND I TO THEM.

THE AFFIRMATION THAT WILL
INFLUENCE THE THOUGHTS OF OTHERS

If, for any reason, it becomes necessary to influence the thoughts of others, this affirmation is tailored to fit your individual needs. And by influencing a person's thoughts, you directly influence a person's actions.

To be effective, this affirmation must be used at a time when the person you wish to influence is asleep. First, say your affirmation. Follow your affirmation by directing your instructions to the subconscious mind of the person sleeping.

> I possess a power that is unrestricted by time and space. My thoughts are strong and all powerful. I command that the subconscious mind of   (name)   hear and obey my Cosmonomic instructions, now!

(Now, talk directly to the sleeping, subconscious mind.)

THE PSYCHIC DECLARATION THAT
AFFIRMS YOUR PERFECT HEALTH

Your present state of health is undoubtedly good, and you want to keep it that way. The power-packed declaration that follows is but another Cosmonomic tool that you can use to maintain a constant flow of psychic power that will energize and revitalize your own physical body every minute of every day.

> I am a perfect child of the Creative Force of all nature. I am surrounded by a wall of Cosmonomic Power, and nothing that is not of good can enter my world.

KEEP YOUR PERSPECTIVE.
ALL AREAS OF YOUR LIFE ARE INTERRELATED

Do not make the mistake of concentrating all of your Ultra-Cosmonomic power to achieve only one goal. If you have wealth but no friends, no love, success, or happiness, your riches will bring nothing but grief.

If you are ill, you cannot enjoy all of the bountiful blessings of life. Riches, perfect health, love, success, and happiness are all interrelated. If you achieve one thing and ignore the rest of the rewards that can be yours you have, in effect, failed. Cosmonomics is balance, harmony, and peace. Do not accept less and do not expect less.

Read on! Chapter Six will reveal more powerful secrets that will give you the peace, harmony, and plenty that are yours upon command.

Chapter Six

POWER YOUR WAY TO LOVE, HAPPINESS, AND PROTECTION FROM EVIL WITH UNIVERSAL MIND MAGIC

This chapter is one of the most powerful in this book. It is also one of the most mystic chapters you will ever read. You will learn new and advanced methods that will focus and direct the flow of Universal Mind power that is at your disposal upon command.

This chapter will reveal how you can transform your entire environment to make it what you want it to be. The same power that keeps the universe functioning smoothly and in its proper

137

order is the same power that is going to give you love, happiness, and protection from evil.

THE ANCIENT MYSTICS LEARNED THAT THE "COSMOS THOUGHT FORCE" WAS A POWERFUL AND VERY WELCOME OCCULT TOOL

Mystics have historically found themselves fighting on the side of the weak and the infirm. Pitting themselves against the rich and the powerful, the ancient wise men found themselves the victims of persecution—persecution which inevitably led to the dungeon.

The feudal lords stripped the mystic of his potions and talismans, thinking that without these occult tools, the mystic would be powerless. And for awhile he was!

Legend states that it was while incarcerated in a dark, damp dungeon cell that a mystic discovered the power of a "cosmos thought force." With nothing to wile away the hours, the mystic experimented with the only tool he had available—his mind. The imprisioned wizard soon learned that with his mind only, he could bend the thoughts of his jailers to do his will. His freedom was assured.

This chapter will teach you to gain the freedom of the mystic. There should be no more dungeons of despair for you! The power of your mind will soon release you from unhappiness and frustration. All of the love and happiness that you can handle will soon be yours upon command.

YOU HAVE PROBABLY ALREADY BEEN THE VICTIM OF AN EVIL COSMOS THOUGHT FORCE

Have you ever experienced:

- deep mental depression for no apparent reason?
- a rash of nightmares or sleepless nights?
- you just can't keep your mind off of a person you do not like?
- fear of dangers that never materialize?
- unexplained nervousness and loss of appetite?

If you have experienced any of these symptons, then you've probably been the unwilling victim of a negative thought force. But this important Cosmonomic chapter will relieve you of the unwanted curses that are being thrown at you daily. You will soon build a wall of protection around yourself that no evil thought dare penetrate.

HOW DONALD G. BROKE THROUGH THE COSMOS THOUGHT FORCE OF AN EVIL, VINDICTIVE WOMAN

Donald G. was interested in Gladys only as a girl friend, not as a wife. He enjoyed their many dates and the fun they had together, but he was not in love with Gladys, and he was not about to give up his "swinging bachelor" type of existence for marriage.

When it became obvious that Gladys was becoming too serious, Donald broke off the relationship.

"I was honest with Gladys from the very beginning," he said. "I told her that I was happy as I was and had no intention, at least for the time being, of becoming attached to just one woman. Gladys thought that was great! She didn't want to become tied down either. 'My career comes before marriage,' she told me.

"Gladys seemed like such a wonderful woman, and it wasn't until I broke off our relationship that I realized what an evil, vindictive person she really was."

Donald thought that Gladys would accept his rejection in an adult manner and that would be the end of the matter. He was totally unprepared for the tumult that was about to build around him.

"Gladys began calling me on the telephone every night. I just could not believe her foul language nor the intense hatred that she had built up against me.

"An opportunity arose to transfer to another city, and I believed that fate had personally stepped in to finally rid me of Gladys. I was mistaken.

"I adjusted quickly to my new environment in Nebraska, but things just went haywire. Everytime I tried to concentrate on my work, I would find myself thinking of Gladys. I lost my appetite and steadily lost weight. I was physically and mentally tired, but rather than experiencing a good night's rest, I'd toss and turn. I would get up in the morning more tired than when I had gone to bed. A physical exam at the doctor's turned up no explanation for my steady slide downward.

"My boss finally called me into his office to ask me if there was anything wrong that he could help with? 'I'm very disappointed in your job performance, and if it doesn't improve, I'm afraid I'm going to be forced to look for another man to fill your job.' "

Donald felt rather silly, but he blurted out the whole story to his boss. Luckily for Donald, his employer recognized that he was being unmercifully battered by the tidal wave of a very negative but powerful Cosmos thought force. Donald was shown how to build a wall of protection around himself and to send the unwanted thought force back to its originator.

Donald did send the Cosmos thought force back to Gladys. And when he did, Gladys became only a statistic when she leaped from the roof of her apartment building.

No, Donald did not make Gladys jump to her death. He only returned her own thoughts back to her. Gladys, and no one else, was responsible for her own misfortune. She planted her own seeds and reaped her own harvest.

HOW TO PROTECT YOURSELF FROM
AN EVIL COSMOS THOUGHT FORCE

In the progress of life you will undoubtedly meet hateful, revengeful people such as Gladys and you should be prepared to instantly protect yourself from their mental attacks against you—before any damage is done.

Universal Mind furnishes you with just the protection you need—a solid wall of psychic energy that drives away the evil but accepts the good.

HOW TO BUILD YOUR PROTECTIVE WALL
OF PSYCHIC ENERGY

You need only to perform this magical ritual once to build your wall of protection. After performing this ritual, a few simple words will ward off any future psychic attacks.

Before you begin your ritual, purchase a small box of clean sand from any pet store (the boxed sand that is used in bird cages or in the bottom of fish aquariums is ideal for the purpose of your ritual).

When the sand is ready and you are in an appropriate location, use the sand to mark off a perfect square. Each side of the square must be exactly four feet.

When the perfect square has been drawn with your sand, place a chair within the square. The chair must be placed so that when you sit in it, you will be facing toward the east.

Now sit in the chair. Your back must be straight. Your hands should rest upon your knees with the palms up.

Now relax for a few moments and drive the thoughts of the day from your mind. When your mind is at peace, visualize waves of energy rising from the sand around you. At first you will imagine, or see the energy waves within your mind, but as you observe further, you will see the psychic energy with your physical eyes as well (it appears much the same as the heat waves generated by the asphalt highways).

With the psychic energy waves clearly in view, repeat these words aloud, and with conviction:

> I am now surrounded by the power of Infinite Good. Unless it be for my own benefit, no thought, no power, no force can enter my world. My Cosmonomic consciousness protects me from all evil. I accept only that which will lead to peace, harmony, love, and happiness. And so it is!

You will experience beautiful sensations during this ritual. Many people find it difficult to break off the ritual. They want to continue sitting in their powerful metaphysical square— absorbing the wonderful vibrations of their new wall of protection. Even though it is difficult to break off your new feeling of heavenly rapture, don't sit within your magical square for more than fifteen minutes. If you sit longer than fifteen minutes, the ritual reverses itself and the sand draws all of the energy back from you.

HOW TO DISPOSE OF THE PSYCHIC SAND
USED IN YOUR RITUAL

There are two ways that you may use to dispose of your magical sand. The first method is to sweep up your psychic sand and literally throw it to the wind.

The second method of disposal may prove a bit more exciting. If there is any flower plant around you whose bloom is the color red, sprinkle the sand at the base of the plant. You will soon begin to notice that the blooms become larger in size, but fade in color. This shows simple psychic energy at work.

If at a future time you feel any of the negative symptoms mentioned earlier in this chapter, say this Positive Declaration:

> I am surrounded by the Infinite Power of Good. I reject all thoughts that are not of Good and return them to their own creator.

WHAT IS A COSMOS THOUGHT FORCE?

Simply speaking, a cosmos thought force is the electrical energy that is produced by your physical body and a force that can be measured with scientific equipment.

The occultist knows that this thought force is more than the simple creation of electrical energy. The occultist knows that this psychic/electrical energy can be manipulated and used as a "psychic arm." It is another powerful occult tool that you can use to create a miracle.

HOW YOU CAN USE YOUR OWN POWERFUL
COSMOS THOUGHT FORCE TO BEND OTHERS
TO YOUR WILL

Using your own powerful cosmic thought force is really much easier than you might expect it to be. It is just a matter of using your own ability to concentrate.

Before you begin to use your new found power, first perform a few harmless experiments. A fun way to begin with your experiments is to determine what your friends or family are going to dream about on a particular night. And this is how you do it.

First, within your mind visualize your subject surrounded by pulsating psychic energy. Then, visualize a ray of your psychic energy shooting into theirs. As the two forces collide, so to speak, issue your command. For an example. "Ruth, you will dream of fire engines tonight." Then, mentally cut the energy ray loose. You have now placed a cosmos thought within Ruth's energy field. The thought will remain in the psychic field where you placed it until it manifests itself. You can smile when Ruth tells you, "I had the craziest dream about fire engines last night!"

Another harmless experiment is to follow the same visualization procedure so that the person to whom you are directing your psychic energy calls you on the telephone or any other such bidding.

As you gain in confidence, use the power of your Cosmonomic thought force for more serious purposes. Is someone ignoring you? Then command that they find you appealing. Do you desire a raise in pay? Command that your employer recognize your true worth.

REMEMBER THESE IMPORTANT
PSYCHIC RULES

To use your Universal Mind thought force effectively to influence the thoughts and actions of others follow the same mental rules as in your experiments.

1. *Visualize the person you want to influence.*
2. *Visualize* your psychic power ray entering their psychic field.
3. *Command* the response that you want to achieve.
4. *Visualize* your psychic ray gun shut off.
5. *Wait* patiently for your miracle. It will happen at the right time and in the proper manner so that you receive the maximum benefit possible.

HOW KAREN X. USED HER POWERFUL
COSMIC THOUGHT FORCE TO LAND A ROLE ON BROADWAY

Karen X. is a fictitious name, but her story is true. In fact, at one time, her story was mentioned in a national publication.

Karen was very much like any other star-struck girl on the outside, but inwardly she seethed with psychic energy.

Karen auditioned and auditioned, but she was never offered a role upon the stage. Karen strongly suspected that it had largely been determined before the auditions who might receive the parts in the play. Karen was discouraged, but she certainly did not give up.

Auditions were to be held for a new Broadway musical. Karen knew that she would be ideal for at least one of the minor roles. But what could she do to ensure that she got the part? This is what Karen did!

On the evening before the tryouts, Karen visualized the play's producer and director within her mind. She then commanded that they intuitively be drawn to her and that she be given a fair chance at the part. Karen got the part, and has since reached super-star status.

HOW EUGENE Z. USED HIS POWERFUL UNIVERSAL MIND THOUGHT FORCE TO REGAIN THE INHERITANCE THAT HE HAD BEEN CHEATED OUT OF

Eugene Z. had spent the majority of his life in the merchant marine. He loved the sea and intended to continue sailing until he was forced to retire.

His widowed mother was quite wealthy. She could buy anything she wanted. Mrs. Z. was never lonely. "I think mother belongs to every club in the world," Eugene once told me.

Eugene was shocked when his mother died. He had not been informed that her health had been deteriorating for months before her death. Why he hadn't been notified became apparent soon after his mother's funeral.

"When the lawyer read mother's will, I couldn't believe it! I wasn't even mentioned in the will. A woman who was a bare acquaintance of mother's received the entire estate. If that was mother's true wish I would have accepted the whole thing without question, but it didn't seem reasonable that an entire estate would be left to a woman known to mother for only a few months."

Eugene did some investigation and found that the woman mentioned in the will had been a part-time nurse to his mother during her last illness. There were witnesses that swore that undue pressure was put on Eugene's mother to change her will. Those who knew her best doubted that she was a rational woman at the time she changed her will. The law courts upheld the validity of the will, but Eugene had just begun to fight for what he knew was rightfully his.

"After I had lost the court fight," Eugene later said, "I decided to use the only weapon I had available—a Cosmonomic thought force.

"I returned to sea, but everynight I pictured that woman's face in front of me. I commanded nightmares, nervousness, fright. But most of all I commanded honesty. When I returned home after four months at sea, mother's property was mine.

"During my absence, Mary (the beneficiary), began to drink heavily. She then turned to drugs. No matter what she tried, she could not escape the torment that I had cast upon her. In desperation she went to mother's lawyer and confessed everything.

"Mary did receive a jail sentence for the fraud she had perpetuated, but upon my plea for mercy, Mary's sentence was suspended. I didn't want revenge, I only wanted justice. When I received what was rightfully mine I withdrew the cosmos thought force from Mary's world.

"Mary instantly felt reborn. She believed her new health and happiness was due to her cleansing of conscience. I knew it was only because I removed my curse from her. But regardless, justice was done.

HOW COLOR CAN BRING LOVE
HEALTH AND HAPPINESS INTO YOUR LIFE

Color plays a much larger role in life than that of which you are consciously aware. Color plays a subtle influence in many, if not all of your decisions.

You use color words in your slang expressions, probably without conscious thought. Do expressions such as these sound familiar?

- I feel blue
- I'm in the pink of condition.
- I feel green around the gills.
- I was so angry I could see red.

Slang yes, but also psychic expressions from the subconscious, higher you. I am going to reveal how you can use color to psychically influence others and how to make miracles happen in an almost unbelievable manner.

HELEN G. USED HER COSMONOMIC COLOR CODE AND WAS MARRIED IN ONE WEEK

Helen G. was a widow. She had had a happy first marriage and saw no reason why she shouldn't enjoy a second happy marriage. She had met a lot of men, but there was just not the mutual attraction or respect that would lead to a solid marriage. Helen wanted a husband, but she did not want just any husband. She was determined that her second marriage would be even happier than the first.

When Helen met Oliver the fireworks went off inside of her, but Oliver was a confirmed bachelor. Using both her intuition and her common sense, Helen sized Oliver up accurately enough to know that she could use color to her advantage in winning him.

Helen knew that Oliver was an intellectual who loved his peace and harmony. Helen also knew that she needed to make Oliver aware of her own attributes in a silent, psychic way. And she did.

Oliver, the confirmed bachelor, went to Helen's for dinner on a Tuesday evening. Before the next Tuesday arrived Oliver had popped the question and he and Helen eloped.

I last saw them at their fifth wedding anniversary party. They were still acting like newlyweds. "I've never been happier," Helen whispered in my ear.

HOW TO USE YOUR OWN
COSMONOMIC COLOR TABLE

First determine the attribute or personality characteristic you want to develop in yourself or others and fill your physical environment with the proper complimentary color. For example, if you want to draw material prosperity toward yourself begin decorating in the reddish tones of brown. When you go to work try to wear these same colors as often as possible. You'll be amazed at the subtle psychic influences that immediately go to work to fulfill your desires.

If you were to wear the blacker tones of brown you would directly influence the subconscious mind of those around you to believe that you are less than prosperous - or a miser. (Many Cosmonomic followers have found it very advantageous to wear these dull brown colors to high pressure fund raising activities). One student reported, "I wore my dark brown suit to the charity fashion show and I was only asked for money once. The other guys with me were pestered until they gave, and then gave more. When my buddies asked me why I wasn't being bothered, I just smiled and said, 'They don't like the color of my suit.' They laughed, but little did they suspect that I wasn't making a joke, I was telling the truth."

Color	*Its Psychic Influence Upon You Or Others*
Bright Red	This color influences and builds an outgoing personality. It should also be used to increase physical strength, health, and vigor.
Bright Red Mixed	This mixed color will bring out the worst. It inflames the mind and causes, or increases, irritation. It brings out the crankiness in the best of people.

Color	_Its Psychic Influence Upon You Or Others_
Pure Crimson	This is the color of lust. It attracts physical attention, but there is no love in the embrace.
Rose	This tone of red brings out the best. It arouses kindness, gentleness. Its psychic influence causes the person to seek good for others before self.
Pink	Pink expresses all around well-being. It creates confidence, trust, peace, harmony.
Red Orange	Red-orange enhances self-esteem. It pushes away shyness and makes the person feel more aggressive. Too much use of this color leads to egotism and a false sense of superiority.
Red Violet	This tone of red should be used to attract people whom you wish to influence to join clubs, lodges, or societies. It is also the color that can be used to attract a proposal of marriage or partnership.
Sky Blue	This color should be used to bring out a desire for spiritual unfoldment. If you decorate your home in this color, you will produce the image of yourself as a spiritually powerful personality.
Violet	Violet expresses the highest of spiritual feelings, as well as pure spiritual thoughts.
Very Dark Blue	This tone of blue which is mixed with black reflects fears that are steeped in superstition. If, for

Color	*Its Psychic Influence Upon You Or Others*
	any reason, you wish to frighten a person who erroneously believes that any form of occultism is the work of the devil, wear this dark blue color and let him overhear you pronounce a simple affirmation or incantation. He will literally run from your presence.
Blue Gray	"I feel blue today," appropriately describes the influences that this color produces upon those surrounded by it.
Purple	Purple produces a love of ceremony. For those who do things in an unorganized manner, purple will straighten the matter out. it will produce the desire to do things methodically and in a proper order. It also brings out the desire for neatness and cleanliness in one's physical environment.
Clear Blue	If you want to produce a sense of justice, morality, or a strong sense of right or wrong, this is the color for you. It is very difficult for a person to tell a lie when surrounded by this color. Want someone to confess bad or unethical behavior? This color will induce the desired "cleansing of conscience."
Light Yellow	If you want to stimulate the mind, appear intellectual or to give off the aura of "the teacher," use this color in abundance.
Bright Yellow	This is definitely not the color to have around hyper-active

Color	Its Psychic Influence Upon You Or Others
	children or adults. This color intensifies their nervousness and causes the mind to work overtime. This tone of yellow infers a very logical mind—a mind ruled by intellect rather than the emotions. This yellow is also conducive to creating a desire to make long-range plans. It shows perseverance.
Gold	Gold reveals a love of pure knowledge. Its dominating influence produces an illusion of the religious teacher, religious philosopher—an individual who seeks the truth in all things.
Yellow Orange	Want to seek a compromise? Want to finally settle an argument or erase hard feelings? If so, you want to use this color abundantly. If you want to discuss a problem but do not want to argue about it, then this again is the color for you.
Mixed Green	Produces a feeling of poor health, laziness, sluggishness, and lack of ambition.
Light Green	Light green works upon the Cosmonomic subconscious mind to show tolerance, patience, and the love of one's home.
Clear Green	This tone of green really gets the psychic energy which surrounds you moving, and moving fast. It shows healing and tremendous strength of character, love of children.
Forest Green	Want to be asked to an outdoor vacation, a jaunt to the countryside,

Color	*Its Psychic Influence Upon You Or Others*
	mountains or the ocean? Splash this color around and just watch the magical results that it produces. This color also reveals a love of animals and of nature.
Dull Green	The person who is untruthful and holds malice within his heart will surely be drawn to this less than good tone.
Clear Reddish Brown	This color shows prosperity and material generosity.
Dull Brown	This color is a subconscious signal that this person is experiencing poverty, or has a tremendous fear of poverty. It shows greed and miserliness.
Gray	Negative in all respects—most usually of thought.
White	This "non-color" is one of the most important and allusive colors that you'll encounter. It can either mean purity, spiritual attainment, or complete neutrality.
Black	Black does not denote death nor the desire for death. Tradition has influenced you to believe black to be the color of mourning, and it can be. But more usually in Cosmonomic color vibrations, black denotes hatred and a desire for revenge.

GENERAL COLOR INTERPRETATIONS

You most probably noticed while reading your Cosmonomic Color Table that certain tones followed generally predictable characteristics. The reds are the physical colors, the blue the spiritual colors, yellow the mental tones, and greens the emotional colors.

If you desire to attract any of the positive attributes that these colors denote, surround your home and fill your wardrobe with the appropriate colors. As your desires change, change the colors around you.

THE COLORS THAT OTHERS WEAR ARE
SECRET COSMONOMIC SIGNS THAT CAN BE READ BY YOU

Why do the people around you wear the colors that they do? Why is each person's home decorated in colors unique to himself? You, as a Universal Mind student already know why. Subconsciously every person chooses to wear, or to decorate with the colors that reveal his true personality.

If you like what you see, help the person along as best you can, but if they show you a negative or selfish personality, beware! This is the time for you to wish them well, but by all means build your psychic wall around yourself and let the negative influences trying to break through your wall of protection go right back to their rightful owner.

COLOR CAN MAKE ANY WISH A REALITY

Patience, common sense, and Univeral Mind power work together to allow your use of color to create a miracle. The only word of caution that I would offer is make sure you really want what you are using your colors to attract, because it really does work. Thousands of people have used the Cosmonomic color knowledge to create miracles and to achieve success. The most recent case history that has come to my attention concerning the power of Cosmonomic color comes from Andrea S., who lives in a large city of northern California.

HOW ANDREA S. USED HER COSMONOMIC
COLOR KNOWLEDGE TO QUADRUPLE
HER BUSINESS IN JUST ONE YEAR

Andrea S. was making a fairly good living from the employment agency that she owned, but it could certainly not have been considered as a phenomenal success story by any means. Andrea's salary had averaged $1200 a month for the year prior to her introduction to Cosmonomic color codes. After her first year of practicing the art of Cosmonomic color, her salary was $60,000 a year—more than four times her previous $14,400 per year salary. How did she do it? Easily!

"I was always fascinated by colors," Andrea wrote, "but until I learned the psychic power of color through my study of Universal Mind I was not aware of the tremendous influence that colors played in every person's life. I am living proof that colors can work miracles."

This is how Andrea used color to attain a yearly salary of $60,000.

Andrea's small employment agency was making a living for her, but it was a one woman operation that meant hard work and long hours. Andrea knew of the tremendous demand for skilled employees in her city, but prospective employees or employers were not utilizing her employment facility to the degree that the labor market was demanding.

Though Andrea could hardly afford the expense, she redecorated her office in reddish brown, bright yellow, and red orange (prosperity, intelligence and self-assurance). Within days Andrea experienced a dramatic increase in the number of employers requesting her services to furnish them competent, qualified employees.

Andrea also had many job seekers at this time, but they were being turned down for jobs after being interviewed by prospective employers. "The people were qualified, but turned down for jobs," she said.

Andrea continued her story:

"I had proven the psychic power of color to myself after I redecorated my office. It grew from my one woman operation to a point where I employed four fulltime girls to help in the office work.

"Prospective employers were paying me a fee to find them qualified employees. Job seekers were paying me a fee to find them lucrative positions; and yet, I just couldn't get prospective employer and prospective employee together in a mutually acceptable manner."

Andrea finally had a psychic hunch. "I've got to instruct my clients as to what colors to wear to their job interviews!" Andrea did, and her business quadrupled.

DON'T LET THE POWERFUL
USE OF COLOR BACKFIRE ON YOU

Anything is good if it is not extreme. Very few mistakes can be made if you use common sense and the power of Universal Mind. These are two very important things to remember: *Common sense and Cosmonomic power!*

Andrea used her color knowledge in a successful and common sense manner, but this is what happened to Elaine E. when she forgot to use her common sense.

HOW ELAINE E. SUFFERED THE
CONSEQUENCES WHEN SHE FORGOT
TO USE HER COMMON SENSE

Elaine wanted a husband more than anything in the world. Elaine erroneously believed that the way to snag a husband was by arousing male sexual passion. She didn't take the time to realize that a good marriage does not evolve from the bedroom only.

Elaine took out her color chart and studied it. She decorated her apartment in dark crimson, blacks, and reds. When she invited Glen over for dinner, she made sure that her new dress and even the wine to be served with dinner were the shades of red that would best suit her very organized plans.

Elaine found that she had been successful in arousing passion. Before Elaine could serve Glen the gourmet dessert that she had prepared, she was raped. No, Glen was not the husband for Elaine, and it was a hard way for Elaine to learn a valuable lesson—"Don't plant the seeds unless you're willing to accept the harvest"!

HEALTH, WEALTH, SUCCESS, AND
HAPPINESS IS MORE THAN LUCK

Through habit, most of you say that any fortunate incident in life is good luck. It's perfectly acceptable to use the word luck, and I'm going to use that very word throughout the remainder of this book. But as an accomplished Universal Mind expert, you have come to realize that your good fortune is not a matter of luck. Your good fortune is the direct result of a psychic force that you have put into action. This true Universal Mind principle should be deeply lodged within your conscious as well as your sub-concious mind. I will be using the word luck as a matter of convenience. You must realize that the word luck has deeper metaphysical significance.

HOW TO DETERMINE YOUR
OWN LUCKY NUMBERS

Your lucky numbers are easily discovered, and by following the metaphysical rules I am about to reveal and with a little elementary arithmetic, the secret is yours! Remember, you have more than one lucky number.

Step one: Write down your birthdate
February 13, 1932, as an example

Step two: Change your birthdate to read:
2-13-32 (month, day, year)
(These are your first three lucky numbers)

Step three: Your master lucky number is revealed by ad-ding the numbers together:
$2 + 13 + 32 = 47$
47 is your luckiest of numbers.

Step four: Add the lucky number (47) from Step three in this manner:
$4 + 7 = 11$
Eleven is a lucky number.

Step five: Add the lucky number from Step four as follows:
$1 + 1 = 2$
Two is a lucky number.

You have now discovered six of your lucky numbers: 2, 13, 32, 47, 11, and, again, 2. Your master or luckiest number was revealed in Step three.

Three additional numbers can be discovered by doing another simple calculation.

I began the step to follow in finding your lucky numbers by using the hypothetical birthdate of February 13, 1932. Let's continue with the same birthdate (you should be using your own birthdate, of course).

February 13, 1932 is again rewritten as 2-13-32. These numbers, as you discovered in step three equal 47. It is now that one, two, or three new and powerful lucky numbers can be discovered. The total number added together (in this instance 47) must be divided by the number of the day of the week upon which the birth occurred. February 13, 1932 fell on a Saturday, which is the seventh day of the week. (Most readers will assume that Sunday is the seventh day of the week, but a quick glance at your calendar will show you otherwise).

Divide the 47 by 7.

47 divided by 7 = 6, with a remainder of 5.

The new lucky numbers are 6 and 5. The third lucky number (if it has not already been discovered in earlier steps) is found by adding the 6 and the 5. In this case the number is 11.

HOW TO USE YOUR LUCKY NUMBERS

Quite obviously if you want to use your lucky numbers at the race track, they must be the lucky numbers that are equal to or less than the number of horses in the race. But what happens when you have several numbers that are below, say, ten? You can't bet on each lucky number and expect to win any money. This is where you must rely on the prosperity rituals, affirmations, and chants that have been given in earlier chapters. Those mystic tools will reveal what horses you should bet on and in which race.

THE MAGICAL RITUAL THAT GIVES
YOUR LUCKY NUMBERS GREATER COSMONOMIC POWER

Your lucky numbers are lucky, but you can make them even luckier!

Write each of your lucky numbers on a small piece of paper (one number only on each paper). When this has been completed, find a safe and suitable container in which the papers can be burned (a fireplace, barbeque, and the like are safe containers).

Your cosmic papers should be burned one at a time. As they burn, you must repeat with absolute conviction this powerful Universal Mind affirmation:

I entrust unto the sky my most sacred numbers.
I know that my numbers have been placed within the bank of all good and all prosperity. I can withdraw my investment from the Bank of Prosperity at will, and with interest. There is no limit to the funds which I may withdraw from the never ending source of all prosperity.
And so it is!

HOW MARLENE D. USED HER NINE LUCKY NUMBERS TO WIN OVER $10,000

Marlene loved to gamble, but had never experienced the joy of winning any large amount of money. Every two or three months Marlene and her friends would go to Nevada to spend a weekend at the gaming tables.

Marlene rarely played Keno—it just wasn't exciting enough for her gambling instincts. But just prior to her last visit to the gambler's paradise, Marlene learned her nine Cosmonomic lucky numbers.

We had just checked in at _____, and before I even went to my room, I stopped at the Keno window and played a seventy-cent nine spot. When the numbers had been called for the next game, I just leaned against the counter and screamed. I had won over $10,000.

HOW TO USE YOUR LUCKY NUMBERS

Lucky numbers are good for much more than gambling. They reveal the dates within any month that you are most likely to find success. Your lucky dates or numbers are good times to begin new projects, new businesses, to begin vacations, and the like. Numbers play a great role in your life. Watch them and use them wisely. They can be used to pay huge dividends, not only in material success, but in finding happiness and love as well.

HOW YOU CAN FORECAST YOUR LUCKY DAY

You have probably noted from the past that good things frequently happen to you on the same day of the week and that negative influences occur more often on one day of the week than another. This happens because you are born to live within a series of cycles. One of these cycles is a seven day or weekly cycle.

The most traumatic event of your life was being born. You were cast from the comfortable, secure world of your mother's womb to suddenly find yourself in a harsh and alien world. Of course you don't remember this traumatic experience, but because of it, the day of the week upon which you were born is the unluckiest day of all.

Your luckiest day of the week, or the beginning of the weekly cycle that follows you throughout your entire life began three days prior to your birth. If, for example, you were born on a Friday, Tuesday is your lucky day. If you were born on Wednesday, Sunday is your luckiest day.

Casual observation upon your part will soon convince you that you do have a very lucky as well as a very unlucky day within each week. You will discover that even your health fluctuates with this cycle concurrently with the physical cycle that was revealed to you in Chapter Four.

Hopefully you have followed the instruction and revelations given to you in this chapter and have already used its power to make your dreams come true. But don't stop now! The next chapter will teach you additional Universal Mind secrets.

Want to test your new found Universal Mind power with an ordinary deck of playing cards? If you do, simply turn the pages.

Chapter Seven

PUT YOUR MIRACULOUS UNIVERSAL MIND POWER INTO ACTION WITH A DECK OF ORDINARY PLAYING CARDS

If you are unsure of the answers given to you through your own intuition or the rituals that you have followed throughout this book, this chapter will give you visible evidence that you are in touch with the great Universal Cosmonomic Mind.

This occult tool that you will learn to use reveals the miraculous signs or cosmic codes that advise you of the future — Cosmonomic codes that can lead you upon a road of life that ensures happiness, wealth, and good health.

A DECK OF PLAYING CARDS GIVES
ALL THE ANSWERS

As you now know, your own psychic power lies deep within your mind, waiting to serve you and to reveal the future.

Previous chapters have taught you how to conquer all obstacles that have kept any of your desires from you, but in the meantime, you can check on the wonderful things that are still to come by looking at the miraculous secrets of the future that are revealed to you by Universal Mind.

ANCIENT EGYPTIAN ADEPTS HID THEIR
SECRET KNOWLEDGE IN PLAYING CARDS

There was a time in the ancient past that Egypt was no longer able to withstand her invaders and prepared to die honorably. It was then that the Egyptian Adepts held a great assembly to arrange how their secret knowledge could be saved.

At first they thought of entrusting their secrets to virtuous men who would pass the knowledge from generation to generation.

But one priest observed that virtue was difficult to find. He proposed that the secret knowledge from the Book of Life be confided to vice, rather than virtue, virtue being fragile at its best.

This opinion was adopted, and the game of vice chosen to hold the secrets of the Egyptian mystics was playing cards.

The design of playing cards has changed a great deal since those days in ancient Egypt, but today's modern design has not cancelled the occult significance of each playing card, nor has it lessened its value in foretelling the future.

CARDS SPEAK IN UNIVERSAL COSMONOMIC CODE

Man is physical, but he is psychological. He is physical and psychological, but he is also spiritual.

Under the stresses of modern civilization, these aspects of man have grown apart as if they were incompatible. Man is no longer an integrated whole. While there may be unity in politics, religion, the arts, and the sciences, it is individual man who suffers the chaos of his own disunity.

Playing cards are an occult tool that can show you how to become a unified individual. There need not be chaos or wishes unfulfilled, for the cards speak to those with the Cosmonomic ear to hear.

HOW THE CARDS POINT TO MIRACULOUS SIGNS

Each card within a playing desk has a mystical meaning. These mystical meanings are the signs from the infinite Universal Mind. They answer every question of the past, the present, or the future.

The cards can be consulted about your physical world, your emotional or your spiritual world. And the signs reveal the answers to your every question.

THE CARDS FORETELL, THEY DO NOT COMPEL

You will undoubtedly consult the cards to determine what will occur in the future, and the cards will foretell the future. But they do not compel.

Cards are an occult tool to understand the past, see the present, and foretell the future. But the signs of the future that are revealed through the cards does not mean that the future foretold cannot be changed. It can be changed! And it should be changed if you are dissatisfied with what the future holds. Foretelling the future with cards gives you the opportunity to make your future exactly what you want it to be.

If you are happy with what the cards foretell, continue as you are. If you do not like what the cards show your future to be you are not compelled to accept it. You have ample warning to change your life so that the unacceptable events do *not* happen.

HOW TO ACQUIRE YOUR DECKS OF CARDS

Two separate decks of cards are required if you are to know all and to see all.

One deck of cards is your Unity of Man deck. With this deck, you will be given instant signs as to the physical, psychological, and spiritual state of yourself or of any other individual.

The second deck of cards is your Wheel of Fortune deck. It will reveal the past, present, and future. This deck will reveal the answers to any question you ask of it.

When you purchase your two decks of fifty-two playing cards, make sure that the seal has not been broken on the packs. The two decks must be identical. They must be new and never before used in any card game.

HOW TO MAKE YOUR CARDS A MAGIC DECK

You should sit alone, and be uninterrupted as you build your two magic decks of cards.

Remove the decks of playing cards from their packages, and lay them side by side upon the table.

Remove the two jokers from the deck on your right and put them on the deck to the left.

This deck on the right is now your Wheel of Fortune deck.

Turn this deck over so that it is now face up.

At the bottom of each card you must print your initials. If the cards are so designed that the bottom of the card cannot be identified, print your initial anyway. Your initials will always identify the bottom of the card.

When your initials have been placed on each card, lay them aside. You will soon be using this magical deck to foretell the future.

THE UNITY OF MAN DECK

Your Wheel of Fortune deck has now been completed and laid aside.

The deck of cards which remain in front of you will soon become your Unity of Man deck.

Pick up this deck of cards. It contains fifty-two playing cards and four jokers (two jokers that came with the deck plus the two jokers added from the other deck).

The only cards that you are to keep from this deck are:

Four jokers
The ace of hearts, clubs and diamonds
The two of hearts, clubs and diamonds
The three of hearts, clubs and diamonds
The four of hearts, clubs and diamonds
The five of hearts, clubs and diamonds
The six of hearts, clubs and diamonds
The seven of hearts, clubs and diamonds

All spades, plus the remaining hearts, diamonds, and clubs should be thrown away.

Your Unity of Man deck now consists of twenty-five cards.

Take the twenty-five cards of this deck and print your initials at the bottom of each card in the same manner as with the Wheel of Fortune cards.

You will soon use this magic deck to know the real personality of any person you seek to inquire after.

No matter what a person may say, no matter how he outwardly acts, your Unity of Man cards will reveal what he really is. No secrets can be withheld from you. The cards will reveal all.

THE POWERFUL RITUAL THAT WILL MAKE
THE CARDS SPEAK TO YOU

Rest your right hand upon your Wheel of Fortune deck and your left hand upon your Unity of Man deck.

Repeat these powerful words:

I stand before the throne of infinite Universal Mind. The signs of all there is to know are now revealed to me in absolute truth.

The seven angels who stand before the throne bear witness to my miraculous power.

Gabriel, Michael, Daniel, Raphael, Camael, Zadkiel, and Zaphiel guard me against falsity. My Cards will speak the truth forevermore.

And so it is!

HOW TO CARE FOR YOUR CARDS

Your magical cards are now yours and yours alone. They can only be used by you.

The cards now contain your vibration or your own unique "feeling." If any other person were to handle your cards, the vibration would be destroyed. The cards are your cosmic link to the Universal Cosmonomic Mind.

There is only one instance in which another person should be allowed to touch your cards.

If you are foretelling the future for another person, they may be allowed to cut the cards. This is the only time that your cards may be touched by another person.

When your cards are not in use, they should be wrapped in velvet and stored in your own secret place.

Remember, keep your two decks of cards separated. If they are ever mixed together, or stored together, their power is lost and they must be thrown away.

HOW EDEN G. DISCOVERED THAT
A MAN LOVED HER

Eden G. was one of those shy, sensitive students when I first met her. She rarely asked questions and seldom spoke to the other students. I was hoping that at least one technique would help overcome her shyness so that she could enjoy people and make new friends.

Eden looked like a middle-aged housewife when she began to learn how to foretell her future. She was sensible looking, but there was nothing that made her stand out from faceless humanity.

After but a few attempts, Eden began to dress differently. She looked years younger and had become the center of attention in her adult education class.

I asked Eden what it was that had caused such a notable change in her.

"Well," she said. "I was always a lonely person. I just never felt like I really belonged anywhere."

Eden was like many people. She felt constant conflict within herself. She felt a divided person with her physical, psychological, and spiritual worlds seeming to go in opposite directions.

"I knew that I had to become a whole person, a unified being," she said.

Eden used her Unity of Man cards and received a revelation.

"I spread my cards and began looking for the signs that would explain my predicament and solve my problems. When I read the cards I could see where I stood on each plane of my development. I could see what caused me to feel the way I did, and I could see how to correct it to my benefit. Once I saw the problem, I knew the solution."

Eden told the class that she had used her Wheel of Fortune cards also, but didn't want to share what her cards foretold until it actually happened.

It wasn't long before Eden was talking to her classmates again.

"I wanted to be loved like anyone else, so I asked the cards if there was anyone who loved me. I was surprised when the cards said that a man did indeed love me."

Eden continued to read the cards until they revealed that a man with whom she worked loved her.

"Tom had never given me any indication that he even knew that I was alive," she related.

"The cards told me that he was shy, but that he would reveal his true feelings at a social occasion.

"I had never gone to an office party before, but when I was asked to the most recent one, I accepted."

Eden continued. "I didn't think Tom would be at the party, but he was. He never spoke a word to me until it was almost time to leave the party. He asked if he could drive me home. Of course I said, 'yes.' "

Just as Tom pulled up to the curb at Eden's apartment, the words just flowed from him like a fountain.

"Tom's words were so beautiful that I could hardly believe my ears. There were a lot of words, but I'll always remember, 'I love you.' "

"We sat snuggled together in the car until the sun came up. I never knew that it was possible to be so happy. Right now I'm letting fate take its course," she said.

Her cards had told the truth, and within a few days Eden had entered a new phase of her existence.

I saw Eden a few weeks later.

"Everything is absolutely perfect," she reported. And her radiance bore ample evidence to the new love she had found.

HOW TO USE YOUR UNITY
OF MAN DECK

Remove your twenty-five card deck from its velvet cover and place them on the table before you.

With your right hand, stir the cards. Keep stirring the cards for approximately one minute.

Push the cards together into a neatly stacked deck.

The Shuffle: Shuffle the cards three times.

The Cut: Cut the cards three times, from right to left.

The Spread: After shuffling and cutting the cards three times, deal seven cards face down from right to left.

Now deal a row of seven cards, right to left, above the first line.

Deal a third row above the first two. You now have three rows of seven cards each.

The bottom row will now reveal your physical state of being. The middle will reveal your psychological state, and the top row will show you the sign of your spiritual level of being.

The Key: The key card that will reveal its secrets to you is the center card in each row — the fourth card from the right.

These key cards are now turned face up. The cards must always be turned by grasping the top of the card and turning it downward.

These cards should be then interpreted by consulting the table which follows in this chapter.

The key cards have now revealed the real you. But that is not the end of the message. The cards will reveal much more.

The cards to the immediate right of the key card will reveal what influences are responsible for your present physical, mental, or spiritual state of being.

The cards to the immedite left of the key card will reveal what your future will bring if you continue on your present course.

HOW TO INTERPRET THE CARDS

Your initials upon the cards will show you which cards are up or down.

Those cards with your initials at the bottom are read as down cards. Those cards with your initials at the top are up cards.

READING THE PHYSICAL AND
PSYCHOLOGICAL STATES OF BEING

<u>Card</u>	<u>Interpretation</u>	
	If Up	*If Down*
Joker	Another person has been the beginning of all things.	You are ruled by another who will be the end of all things.
Ace of diamonds	Happiness for him who controls his own passions.	Work, struggles, and sorrows.
Two of diamonds	Union of the male and female or of opposites.	Illness, pain. A dual nature. Is not true to self.
Three of diamonds	Activity and knowledge bear fruit.	A wish to succeed remains a wish.
Four of diamonds	Change through enlightenment.	Energy is misdirected.
Five of diamonds	Material success.	Must make the choice of good or evil.
Six of diamonds	The lovers' card. Advance or recede.	Jealousy, adultery.
Seven of diamonds	Victory	Failure
Ace of clubs	Strength	Weakness
Two of clubs	Be as wise as the serpent, but gentle as the dove.	Deceit

Three of clubs	A new beginning found in social environments	Loneliness
Four of clubs	Justice	Loss, legal problems.
Five of clubs	Success in get-rich schemes.	Does not see that which is useful.
Six of clubs	Life will change dramatically. Things begin anew.	All good things are swept away.
Seven of clubs	Temperance in all things.	Selfishness, greed.
Ace of hearts	Fate obstructs reality.	Bondage to another.
Two of hearts	Willpower overcomes opposition.	Yields to temptation
Three of hearts	Faith, truth, and hope.	Must admit faults to another.
Four of hearts	Failure that is not permanent.	Permanent failure.
Five of hearts	Inheritance. Money from another.	A loved one moves away.
Six of hearts	Healing. The elixir of life.	In need of a physical examination.
Seven of hearts	Complete happiness and harmony. All is well.	Happiness and prosperity will come only with work and perseverance.

HOW TO INTERPRET THE SPIRITUAL
STATE OF BEING

Card	Interpretation	
	If Up	*If Down*
The joker	Spiritual revelation.	False doctrines.
Ace of diamonds	Spiritual attainment.	Duplicity. Does not act as he thinks.
Two of diamonds	The door of the future is open.	Tries to find spiritual bliss in physical passion.

Three of diamonds	Uses spiritual knowledge to change the physical world.	You have descended into material conditions.
Four of diamonds	State of self-realization.	The womb of spiritual truth lies barren.
Five of diamonds	Religion, inspiration.	Loss of faith.
Six of diamonds	Human love. A coming together.	Loss of love. Divorce.
Seven of diamonds	The material world is vanquished by the work of the will.	Poverty. The baser nature reigns.
Ace of clubs	Spiritual strength. Liberation from fear.	Fear. Shyness. Deceit.
Two of clubs	You carry a lighted beacon.	You lead others by false truth.
Three of clubs	Good fortune for all you touch.	You will be cheated by those you respect.
Four of clubs	Spiritual justice, forgiveness.	Hate, envy.
Five of clubs	You will sacrifice for duty.	You will be condemned as guilty.
Six of clubs	Spiritual vision.	Nightmares, spiritual upheaval.
Seven of clubs	Proper physical union. A soulmate.	Recrimination, loss of good will.
Ace of hearts	Rises above temptation.	Suffers the sins of the past.
Two of hearts	Strikes down all who transgress the law.	Great arrogance, egotism.
Three of hearts	There will be inner and outer beauty.	The physical appearance changes.
Four of hearts	Fear of the natural mind.	False radiance. False entry.
Five of hearts	Restoration of spirituality. A sacred union.	Adversity among the sexes.

| Six of hearts | Speaks to the voice within. | Lack of conscience. |
| Seven of hearts | Recognition of immortality. | Fear of death, evil. |

The Unity of Man cards have now revealed where you stand on the ladder of progression in all aspects of your life. The cards have shown the real you.

These cards can also be used to discover what any person in the world is really like. If you are going to read about another person from the cards, state his name before the first shuffle of your cards.

There are instances when a person might ask you to read the cards for him or her. In such a case, the person for whom you are forecasting may cut the cards. The cards must always be cut three times, right to left.

YOUR WHEEL OF FORTUNE CARDS
WILL ANSWER EVERY QUESTION

Your Wheel of Fortune cards will answer your every question. The signs from infinite Universal Mind will be evident in every card. I will teach you to recognize these signs so that in every instance you will be able to foretell the future with accuracy.

You can test your other Cosmonomic powers with the cards. You can see the past, understand the present, and know the future. The truth of the cards is uncanny. The power of the cards seems unbelievable to those who have not been previously initiated into other cosmic code secrets, such as dominos.

WHAT THE SUITS OF CARDS IN
YOUR DECK REPRESENT

The suits of card within your Wheel of Fortune deck represent general influences that govern your card readings. If a preponderance of one suit appears as you spread the cards, it is an indication that the entire card reading should be slanted in that direction.

Clubs:

This is the suit of the laborer. It indicates constant renewal and growth. This suit reflects animation and enterprise, energy and growth. Clubs are association with the world of ideas, also creation in all of its forms—including agriculture. The direction assigned to the clubs is the south.

Hearts:

Hearts are the suit of the priest. Their direction is west. This suit generally indicates love and happiness. Hearts symbolize the subconscious mind, instinct, and the emotions of love and pleasure. Also hearts represent the good life, fertility, and beauty.

Spades:

Spades are the suit of the warrior. This is the suit of misfortune and disaster. It reflects aggression, strife, boldness, and courage. It can also mean hatred, battle, and enemies. The direction of spades is north.

Diamonds:

Diamonds are the suit of the merchant. Their direction is east. They are symbols of the magic arts. Diamonds indicate money, acquisition of wealth, inheritance, and trade.

HOW TO USE YOUR
WHEEL OF FORTUNE CARDS

Your Wheel of Fortune cards should only be used to answer questions of a serious nature. They will not accurately respond to silly or frivolous questions.

Infinite Universal Mind takes all of your questions seriously. And while you are shuffling the cards, Universal Mind works through your subconscious mind to influence the order in which the cards will fall. Each card is a miraculous sign. Each card speaks a total message and yet, it is but one part of the whole.

Before the cards are spread to foretell the future, the card that represents the person asking the question is removed from the deck. This representative card is then placed face up upon the table and left there during the entire reading. At the end of the reading, the representative card is returned to the deck.

The representative cards indicate the physical description of the person asking the question. Eyes that are green, hazel, and the like are considered as brown eyes.

Jacks represent unmarried persons of either sex, and regardless of age.

Jack of diamonds	— Light hair, blue eyes.
Jack of clubs	— Dark hair, blue eyes.
Jack of hearts	— Light hair, brown eyes.
Jack of spades	— Dark hair, brown eyes.

Queens represent married women and widows.

Queen of diamonds	— Light hair, blue eyes.
Queen of clubs	— Dark hair, blue eyes.
Queen of hearts	— Light hair, brown eyes.
Queen of spades	— Dark hair, brown eyes.

Kings represent married men or widowers.

King of diamonds	— Light hair, blue eyes.
King of clubs	— Dark hair, blue eyes.
King of hearts	— Light hair, brown eyes.
King of spades	— Dark hair, brown eyes.

When the representative card has been placed face up on the table, the question you wish the cards to answer should then be asked aloud.

The Stir: The Wheel of Fortune cards should be placed on the table face down and stirred with the right hand in a clockwise direction. The stirring should continue for approximtely thirty seconds. When the stir has been completed, push the cards together into a neat stack.

The Shuffle: The cards must be shuffled exactly three times. The question asked should be repeated once more during this shuffle.

The Cut: The cards are to be cut three times, from right to left.

The Spread: Deal a row of seven cards face down, from right to left.

Now deal a row of five cards, from right to left and place them in a row above the seven cards.

Deal a row of three cards and place them above the other two rows of cards. You now have a row of seven cards, a row of five cards, and a row of three cards.

The Key Cards: The key cards are the center card in each of your three rows. In the bottom row it is the fourth card from the right. In the middle row it is the third card from the right, and in the top row it is the second card from the right.

The key cards are now turned over by grasping the top of the card and turning it downward. (Whenever cards are turned, they must be turned in this same manner — from top to bottom).

It is these key cards that reveal the answer to your question.

HOW TO READ THE WHEEL OF FORTUNE CARDS

The Past: The top row of three cards tells you of the past. The only importance of the past is its relationship to the present. The key card in this row reveals what occurred in the past to bring about the present.

The card to the right of the key card should now be turned. This card upon the right reveals those influences which caused or created the past experience.

When the card to the left of the key card is now turned it reveals the reaction to the past experience — how one handled the situation.

Generally speaking, this row of cards reveals what influenced you in the past to bring you to the present. These cards are telling you why you are now asking the question that you are.

The Present: The center row of five cards reveals the present. It tells you where you are today in relationship to your question. The key card in this row tells you exactly where your question stands as of the exact moment asked.

As you turn the cards to the right of the key card, the influences that have recently been in play will be revealed.

The cards to the left of the key card reveal what you can expect to happen in the near future with respect to your question.

The Future: The key card in this row of seven mystic signs is the answer to your question. This card reveals success or failure, yes or no, prosperity or adversity. Though the key card is the answer to your question, the remaining six cards are signs that explain why your question was answered in the manner that it was.

The three cards to the right of the key card tell you exactly what the forces are that created your answer. If you are happy with the answer to your question, you can look forward to the things that will transpire before your success is granted.

If you do not like the answer to your question, the cards to the right of the key card give you the opportunity to change your pattern of living so that the things foretold do not occur within your life.

Remember, the key card has already answered your question. To understand why the answer is as it is, turn over the card to the far right of the row. Then turn over the card to its left and then the card to the left of this second card. These three cards show specific things that will happen before your expressed desire is manifested.

The three cards to the left of the key card in this row tell you what will happen after your wish has been granted. Failure to heed the signs from the entire row of cards can have sorry consequences, as Jerry H. learned to his own dismay.

HOW JERRY H. FAILED TO HEED THE
CARDS AND LOST EVERYTHING HE OWNED

Jerry H. had learned to read the Wheel of Fortune cards from a pamphlet, and he had become quite good at forecasting the future.

Jerry's only desire was to own his own business, and everything in his life was devoted to that end.

Every night before going to bed, he would spread his cards. Each time that he spread the cards the answer to his question would turn up as *No*.

Jerry paid particular attention to those influences at work in the row of cards revealing the present. He could see that what he was doing in the present would not lead to his owning his own business. And his own common sense revealed the same thing. Jerry was not qualified to operate his own business.

Jerry took business courses at college, he saved his money, and he met a partner with money to spare and an idea for a marketable product.

Jerry spread his cards again. Hurray! The cards revealed that Jerry could now have his own business.

He was happy that the key card in his future row of cards showed success. He studied the cards to the right of the key card in depth. He wanted to know, step by step, what would transpire before his business was formally opened. He totally ignored the cards to the left of his key card. "The only thing I care about is getting my own business. I don't care what happens after that" he said. But he should have cared.

The key card did reveal that Jerry would have his own business, but the cards to the left of the key card told him that after he did get his business he would be faced with bankruptcy and legal actions. And that's exactly what happened.

The product that Jerry and his partner manufactured was faulty and brought injury to a great many people. Legal actions followed. Within weeks Jerry's firm was bankrupt and deeply in debt.

Universal Mind told Jerry what would happen, but he chose to ignore the signs. Jerry's only interest was in satisfying his immediate pleasure and he gave no heed to its consequences.

The moral of Jerry's story is significant. Make absolutely sure that you pay heed to all of the cards and make sure that the consequences of having your wish fulfilled are consequences which lead to prosperity and happiness rather than desolation and gloom.

If unpleasant things are forecast, take the time to make the necessary adjustments to your life so that the cards foretell those things which you desire, and are things that you want to hold on to.

HOW TO INTERPRET YOUR
WHEEL OF FORTUNE CARDS

Each card that you turn over in your spread has a significant meaning. But an accurate forecast can only be achieved if you read the entire row of cards as one whole. Make a story of each row of cards. Each individual card is a sign that reveals but one chapter in your book of life.

The table which follows reveals how you are to interpret each card. If your initials appear at the bottom of the card follow the interpretation under down. If your initials appear at top of the card, follow the interpretation listed under the heading, up.

Card	Interpretation	
	If Up	*If Down*
Ace of clubs	The beginning of something new. An invention, family or journey.	Cancelling a new enterprise. Journey deferred, false starts.
Two of clubs	Courage in embarking on a new venture. Scientific methods prove best. Influence over another. A proud but unforgiving nature.	A good beginning faces failure. Physical suffering. Restlessness and fear.

Card	Interpretation	
	If Up	*If Down*
Three of clubs	Realization of hope, wealth, or power. Caution against pride, arrogance, and partnership. Help from a merchant.	Beware of help offered. Wealth may disappear. Treachery and disappointment.
Four of clubs	Rest after labor. Peace, prosperity, and harmony. A romance, marriage.	Rest after labor. Peace, prosperity, and harmony. A romance, marriage. Generosity. New business opportunities.
Five of clubs	Violent strife, rashness, competition. A lawsuit. Boldness changes things for the better.	
Six of clubs	Success through industry. Advancement in arts and science. Friends are helpful.	Rewards after a delay. Watch for successful enemy.
Seven of clubs	You are in the position of advantage. Competition, but certain success.	Ignorance, pretense. Caution, you are threatened.
Eight of clubs	Too rapid advancement. Hasty communications. Letters of love. Approach to a goal. Journey by air.	Delay. Arrows of jealousy. Stagnation in business or love.
Nine of clubs	Pause in a struggle. Good health, strength, and power.	Weakness, ill health. Obstacles to be overcome.
Ten of clubs	Power unwisely used. A test of the heart. A problem soon to be solved.	Intrigue and separation. If a lawsuit is pending there is loss.

Card	Interpretation	
	If Up	*If Down*
Jack of clubs	A generous friend or lover will be cruel and brutal. A change of residence, quick departure.	Discord and frustration. Lack of energy. Work interfered with.
Queen of clubs	Practical with money and sound in business judgment. Success in love and home.	Domineering, obstinate, and revengeful. If married, she could become unfaithful.
King of clubs	Agile in mind and body. Honesty, friendliness, passion. This card may mean an unexpected inheritance. A good marriage.	Intolerance, prejudice. Severe and ruthless.
Ace of hearts	The beginning of great love. Beauty and pleasure.	False love. Clouded joy, instability.
Two of hearts	The beginning of a deep friendship or love affair. A balance between good and evil.	False love. Folly, violent passion. Misunderstanding.
Three of hearts	Success and abundance. Good luck.	Too much sensuality. Over indulgence in food or drink.
Four of hearts	Dissatisfaction with material success. Kindness from others.	New relationships now possible. Set new goals.
Five of hearts	Disappointment. Sorrow. Loss of friendship, marriage, or partnership.	Return of past alliances, love, or friendship.
Six of hearts	Happiness coming from the past. A gift from an admirer.	Living too much in the past. Possibility of inheritance.

Card	Interpretation	
	If Up	*If Down*
Seven of hearts	Castles in the air. Imagination has been working overtime. Deception.	Slight success must be followed up. Intelligent selection.
Eight of hearts	May desire to leave material success for something higher. Disappointment in love.	Interest in success. The spiritual is abandoned for the material.
Nine of hearts	Material success. Wishes fulfilled. Good health.	Misplaced reliance. Possible illness.
Ten of hearts	Lasting success. The perfecting of human love.	Loss of friendship. Betrayal. Criminal intents.
Jack of hearts	A young man who is lazy. Can bring a proposition or an invitation.	Sensual, idle; trickery, falsehood.
Queen of hearts	A woman who is a good wife and mother. Honest and loyal.	A perverse, immoral character.
King of hearts	A man skilled in law and trade. He is kind and considerate.	A powerful man, but crafty and violent. Beware of being robbed of money or virtue.
Ace of spades	The power to love or to hate strongly. Possible birth of a child.	Obstacles. Great loss. Infertility.
Two of spades	Tension in relationships. A stalemate. Military friendships.	Avoid impostors. Be generous with sympathy.
Three of spades	Tears, separation, quarreling, Political strife.	Confusion, loss, sorrow.

Card	Interpretation	
	If Up	*If Down*
Four of spades	Rest after war. Relaxation of anxiety.	Renewed activity. Qualified success.
Five of spades	Failure, defeat, slander, unfairness, cruelty.	Empty victory. Attendance at a funeral.
Six of spades	The future will be better. Journey by water. A journey in consciousness.	Stay where you are. Unfavorable issue of a lawsuit or other legal matter.
Seven of spades	A plan may fail. An unwise attempt to take what is not yours.	Possibility of unexpected good. Sound advice.
Eight of spades	Betrayal. Fear to move from a situation. Temporary illness.	New beginning now possible. An impulsive generous nature. Relaxation from fear.
Nine of spades	Suffering, loss, misery. Illness. May mean the death of a loved one.	Patience, unselfishness. Time brings healing.
Ten of spades	Ruin of plans and projects. Defeat in war. Trouble will come in spite of riches.	Overthrow of evil forces. Some success and profit.
Jack of spades	A brave young man. Domineering, but clean of heart.	Extravagance. Bragging. Tyranny over the helpless.
Queen of spades	May represent a widow or one who cannot bear children. Mourning for those who are far away.	Gossip. Deceit. A narrow-minded woman.

Card	Interpretation	
	If Up	*If Down*
King of spades	This is a man who may be a lawyer, judge, officer, or politician. A lawsuit is about to begin.	Distrustful, suspicious. Plotting. Has the power to disrupt.
Ace of diamonds	The beginning of new wealth and material gain.	Miserliness, greed. A false start.
Two of diamonds	The ability to juggle two situations at one time. Recreation. New projects may prove difficult.	Forced gaiety. Inability to handle several situations at the same time.
Three of diamonds	Material success. The master crastsman, the skilled artist. This card rules groups and societies.	Lack of skill. Ignorance. Preoccupation with gain.
Four of diamonds	Gifts, legacy, inheritance. An ungenerous character.	Prejudice and suspicion. The spendthrift. Chance of material loss.
Five of diamonds	Unemployment, loss of home. Loneliness. Dark nights for the soul.	Money regained after severe toil. Charity. New employment.
Six of diamonds	Alms dispensed with justice. You will receive what you deserve.	Jealousy. Bad debts. Gifts given as a bribe.
Seven of diamonds	Unprofitable speculation. Anxiety about a loan.	Impatience. Little gain after much work.

Card	Interpretation	
	If Up	*If Down*
Eight of diamonds	Learning a trade or a profession. A commission. Skill in material affairs.	False vanity, intrigue. Skill turned to cunning.
Nine of diamonds	Wisdom where one's interests lie. Inheritance. A green thumb. Interest in homes and gardens.	Danger from thieves. Cancelled projects.
Ten of diamonds	Riches. Interest in one's family tree. A problem concerning a will or pension. May acquire a house or business property.	Family misfortune. Old people may become a burden. New projects are a poor risk.
Jack of diamonds	A man of upright nature who accepts responsibility. Trustworthiness.	A static nature that is dull, timid, idle, and careless.
Queen of Diamonds	A woman who is generous with her material gifts. Trust of those around.	Mistrust, suspicion. Duties are neglected.
King of diamonds	Success in money matters. A man who is a banker or owner of large properties. A mathematician.	Stupidity. Easy to bribe. If crossed, this man can become a danger.

LET YOUR CARDS BE THE SIGN OF A NEW AND PROSPEROUS LIFE

Practice with your cards until you become an expert. Continue with your activities until you bring yourself into direct contact with the source of Cosmonomic codes — the great Universal Mind. You are moving ever closer to unlimited understanding. Money, love, and health can be yours with the simple flip of a card.

Chapter Eight

PERFECTING YOUR UNIVERSAL MIND POWER TO OPEN NEW DOORS OF EXPRESSION, FULFILLMENT, AND ACCOMPLISHMENT

You are now moving into the last chapter of *Universal Mind* and possibly the most important chapter of the book.

At this point you have learned that you can have all of the love, money, and health that you want — and you probably do! But do you feel that there is still something missing that you just can't put your finger on?

It takes a great deal of emotional and psychological maturity to adjust to your now almost perfect life. It isn't as easy as one might think to move from a world dominated by lack, poor health, and unhappiness to a world filled with plenty, good health and security.

KNOW WHO ARE YOU!

If I were to ask, "Who are you? " your immediate reply would most probably be, "I'm John Jones or I'm Jane Smith."

You are much more than a name. You are a perfect expression of the Great Creative Mind that put the universe into action. And it is because you are this perfect expression that you can perform what some people term "miracles." You really aren't performing miracles, you're only expressing those riches of life that were yours to experience from the moment of birth. Look upon your new found powers as natural powers. There is really nothing supernatural about what you're doing at all. Anyone could do the same things if they were only to realize what a good and powerful person they really were.

HOW TO PLAY THE GAME OF LIFE

We play games first for enjoyment, and secondly to win over our competition. Life is no different.

Life is meant to be enjoyed, and Cosmonomics has taught you how to win over the competition. Let's face it. Most of your competition in life comes from people who care little for the feelings and welfare of others. They step upon one person after another trying to climb the ladder to success. You probably know just such a person at this very moment — a person who has placed a roadblock in your own path of life. Well I'm going to show you how to remove that roadblock and how to knock that person right off his feet.

HOW TO "ZAP" THE PERSON WHO
PLACES A ROADBLOCK IN YOUR PATH OF LIFE

The unleashing of directed occult power is awesome. It can bless your friends and devastate your enemies. The ray guns that appear so frequently in science fiction movies look like a child's toy when compared to the occult power you are now going to use against those people who attempt to impede your walk through life.

First, sit comfortably in a straight-backed chair. Then visualize a picture of the person within your mind. When you have a good, strong picture of your enemy within your mind, move the image so that it is standing six to ten feet in front of you.

You want the person you're going to zap to know exactly why he's going to be punished and where the punishment is coming from. There's nothing wrong with putting a little fear into your enemies. They'll think twice before they try to pull anything else on you.

The image of your enemy is now clear before you. Speak directly to this image. Tell this enemy exactly why you are going punish him.

Sit quietly again for a few moments. Picture the psychic energy within your mind building in strength. Visualize this Universal Mind power as a great ball of light. When this light reaches its zenith — the point where you are just bubbling with energy, lift your right arm and point it at the image of your enemy. Then with great force say, "zap!" You will literally feel this dramatic occult force travel from your head, down the right side of the neck to the right arm, to finally roll off the end of your fingertips. You can watch with satisfaction as the image of your enemy is blasted into a million pieces.

HOW MERILEE M. ZAPPED HER
BOSS AND WON A PROMOTION

Merilee M. worked for a very large corporation. Merilee had exceptional ability, but found it difficult to understand why the men in her department received promotion after promotion while she remained on the same job.

Merilee wasn't a trouble maker and she didn't like to create problems. When Merilee first approached her boss for an explanation as to why she was being passed over for promotions, he became very indignant. "All promotions in our department are strictly upon merit," he told Merilee. She knew that this wasn't true and strongly suspected that the only reason she wasn't promoted was because she was a woman.

Merilee went back to work and began keeping a log of jobs begun and jobs completed. The results showed that Merilee was outperforming every man in the department.

She again approached her boss, but this time Merilee had proof that if merit determined promotions, she should be the next one in line.

Merilee's boss became very belligerent and refused to look at his employee's log. "If you are unhappy here, I'd suggest you look for a new place to work," and stood up and walked out of his office.

Merilee was furious. She was just not about to look for another job, and above all else, she just wasn't about to let that man treat her so unjustly.

That same night, Merill sat down and performed her zap ritual. Merilee later told me what happened as a result of zapping her boss.

"I was still so furious at my boss that when he didn't show up at work the morning after I performed my ritual, I was relieved. I just didn't want to even look at him.

"He still hadn't shown up for work at lunch time. It was about one o'clock when he finally called into the office. He was badly shaken, but unhurt, from a freak accident that had occurred as he was driving to work."

Merilee went on to say that as her boss was driving down the freeway, a truck loaded with bags of cement was crossing the overpass. The bags of cement shifted and fell from the truck to the freeway below. Over a ton of cement had fallen onto the hood of her boss' car. He luckily received only minor bruises as the entire front of his auto was flattened against the asphalt. Coincidence? Merilee didn't think so.

"It was a couple of days after my boss returned to work that he called me into his office," she said.

"Merilee," he said, "I'd like to apologize for my past actions. I really didn't believe that I was treating your unfairly until the other night — the night before I had my accident. All

night I kept waking up thinking about how unfair I had been,
and I had this strange feeling — a fear, really, that I was going
to be punished for having treated you unjustly. When that cement hit my car, the first thing I thought about was you.
"I just want you to know that I've put in for a promotion for
you. I hope you'll forgive me for the way I've treated you in
the past, and I promise it'll never happen again."

Of course Merilee forgave her boss, but as she later said,
"That whole thing could not have been a coincidence. The odds
would be astronomical that he would dream as he did, and then be
involved in such a freak accident just as I zapped him. No, it
wasn't a coincidence. The Universal Mind power really went to
work."

USE A THREE STEP APPROACH TO REACH
YOUR ULTRA-COSMONOMIC POWER LEVEL

The first step in reaching the ultimate satisfaction from your
Universal Mind power is to know what you really want.
·   Surprisingly, few people really know what they want to make
their life happier, but fortunately you have now grown far past
these elementary principles.
The person who is poor in material possessions will probably
say, "More money will make me happier." More money certainly
can bring more happiness into life, but it can't add a thing to your
life if you don't know what you are going to do with it once you get
it. And that leads to the second step in realizing utlimate happiness in your life. Be ready to receive your desires.
Many people cause a miracle to happen, and when it does occur, they don't know what to do with it.
Most psychics, occultists etc., have a tremendous sense of
humor. A fellow psychic teacher was recently telling of a student
who caused a miracle to happen and then was unprepared to accept it. Aside from making a point, I think you'll appreciate the
humor in the story.
Louise H. loved clothes and had always hoped for an enor-
mous wardrobe of clothes — but she thought the likelihood of
ever owning such a collection was remote.

Louise began using chants, invocations, and the like to acquire her heart's desire. It took a couple of months to happen, but when her miracle did occur, she invited her friends over to view the results.

Louise had a small and adequate apartment, but what a surprise when she opened the door to greet her guests. The apartment was stacked with clothes, bolts of cloth, and other such articles. There was barely room for a path to walk from room to room.

When asked what happened, here was Louise's reply.

"Here's the proof that miracles do happen," she said as she pointed about the room. "I chanted for a new wardrobe and got it. The only problem was that I forget to limit its size. I've got so many clothes that I can hardly get from one room to another.

"A friend of mine closed down his clothing manufacturing business and gave his entire stock to me."

No damage was done, and Louise had a great deal of enjoyment in giving away her surplus of clothes, but if you could have seen her apartment, it would have been immediately obvious that Louise was unprepared for her miracle.

The moral of this amusing story? Simply this. Know exactly what you want when you ask for a miracle, and *be prepared to accept it when it appears.*

Step One: Know what you want!
Step Two: Be ready to receive your miracle!
Step Three:: Make your miracle happen!

Step Three is the easiest part of your three step approach to ultimate Cosmonomic satisfaction. This book tells you how to perform your miracle — how to make a mircle happen. It is only you who has the power or the knowledge required to efficiently fulfill Steps One and Two.

You may feel that the three step Ultra-Cosmonomic approach to satisfactory living isn't necessary, but, experience will soon prove to you that there is no other way.

HOW TO EARN THE SPECIAL
ATTENTION OF THE CREATIVE
UNIVERSAL MIND

The creative Universal Mind is ever ready to help any person that calls upon its power, and it does not play favorites. But it does give special attention to those who play the game of life according to the rules.

Every person you meet in life is a teacher. You learn something from every person who crosses your path. But these teachers are only preparing you to advance to an even higher level of learning in the school of life. You learn from your teachers, but it is the principal of the school who determines the curriculum to be taught. The teachers are only assistants in the principal's organization and are picked for their ability to bring out the latent talents among their fellowmen. A good student will pay attention to the assistants, for they have much to teach.

Your own success depends upon your ability to learn from the principal's assistants. Do your best to learn from every experience of your life.

If you learn your Cosmonomic fundamentals as set forth in this book and play life's game according to the rules, you'll win the Principal of the School of Life's personal attention.

There is a special personal interest shown by the Great Creative Mind to those individuals whose striving has earned them a place as first string players in the game of life. The reward for playing the game well is continuing mystic experience.

HOW TO PREPARE YOURSELF
TO RECEIVE A MIRACLE

There is little effort or sacrifice required to perform a miracle, but the deep mystical experience would be worth any price. The striving for Cosmonomic attunement with Creative Mind has been the subject of the previous chapters within this book.

Ancient occult folklore states that the first step in accepting a

miracle is the "purification of the temple." And you have been doing just that since you read the first page of this book. Anything
which improves your health, happiness, or material wealth is a
purification of the temple — you! You are the temple!

Consciously you have been cooperating with the cosmic
forces around you. You have cleansed the temple. As you do your
best to improve all areas of life you have already prepared yourself
to receive a miracle. Little else is required.

ATTUNE YOURSELF TO MYSTIC FORCES

Everything is this book has been directed toward attuning
you with the Creative Universal Mind of all nature. And you are
attuned with these mystic forces whether you realize it or not.
True realization of the mystic forces at work around you is worth
the small price that is needed to pay.

Take a few minutes each day (anytime at your leisure), to
contemplate the mysteries at work around you. Your few minutes
a day can be in the form of meditation, relaxation, or a quiet walk
through the woods. This "quiet time" is signaling the Great
Universal Mind that you are indeed working in conscious
cooperation with the greatest force in the universe — the power of
good. The power of perfect health, happiness, and prosperity.

YOU CANNOT AVOID CONFLICT

I would be untruthful if I were to tell you that Cosmonomics
will free you from conflict for the rest of your life. It won't!

Nothing can prevent conflict. Conflict is an absolute neces-
sity — a vital ingredient that is needed for all growth. If any person
claims that his life is free of conflict, then there is something definitely wrong with the person making such a claim.

It is not conflict that you want to avoid. It is the negative reaction to conflict that you must overcome. All growth begins with
conflict.

Every time you are faced with making a decision you are
faced with mental conflict. It is the conflicts occurring within your
mind that forces you to use your free-will to arrive at a conclusion
or a decision.

A common thread that has run throughout the case histories presented in this book is conflict. There was conflict necessary to create a miracle.

In Chapter Six you read how Eugene won back the inheritance that he had been cheated out of. He miraculously won his battle, but in so doing he quite correctly created conflict by going to court.

The serious student of the miraculous power of Universal Mind soon learns that conflict can be a blessing rather than a curse. It can only become a curse if you consciously allow it to become so. Meet each conflict as an opportunity to learn and grow. Positive reaction to conflict fills your life with the mystical rainbows of health, happiness, and plenty.

BE PREPARED TO FIGHT
FOR WHAT IS YOURS

Cosmonomics has taught you that you have no reason to fear any person in this world. There is no person any more powerful than you are at this very moment. You have a hundred psychic secret weapons at hand to defeat any antagonist, and don't hesitate to use them.

Don't allow yourself to be intimidated by those who hold riches, power, or social position. The power of Universal Mind recognizes every person as an equal, and you can beat the unscrupulous everytime.

WHAT YOU DO WITH YOUR
MIRACLE DEPENDS UPON YOU

I have revealed dozens of methods by which you can perform miracles, but my obligation ceases at that point. I am not responsible for what you do with your miracles as they enter your life by the dozens. It is you who must make the decision as to what you are going to do with your miracles. Miracles do not create happiness — what you do with the miracle does create happiness.

Cosmonomics is giving you the best chance of your lifetime to experience health, happiness, and harmony. And now it's all up to you. Use common sense, compassion, and let your life be ruled by a sense of justice and fair play. That will make you a sure winner in life's race.

RETAIN BALANCE IF
YOU WISH TO SUCCEED

Now that you have embarked upon a new mystical experience of life, you will at times feel so harmonious with the universe, that you will feel tempted to withdraw from the sometimes hectic pace of life. I often feel this same temptation myself — it's a beautiful experience, but impractical in terms of existence.

Like it or not, this is the world in which we live. It is the eternal *now* that is of importance. Make that eternal now an existence of love, health, prosperity, and happiness. You already know how, so perform your chants, rituals, and other observances and make your world exactly what you want it to be.

YOU'RE NEVER TOO OLD TO
EXPERIENCE THE FULLNESS OF LIFE

Your chronological age in years is no hurdle in experiencing the joys of a rich and full life.

It is not unusual to hear, almost daily, people saying that there are many things they would like to accomplish in life, but are now too old. Nothing could be further from the truth.

ALVIN C. BECAME A
FATHER AT FIFTY-TWO

Alvin C. had been a semi-invalid since World War II. He and his wife had wanted children, but the doctors had told him that there was absolutely no chance that he could ever become a father.

Al never gave up hope. When he was 52 years old, his 43 year old wife announced that she was pregnant. The happy couple were thrilled with their perfectly healthy baby girl. No, that isn't the end to an already happy story.

Five years later, the 48 year old Mary announced to the now 57 year old Al that she was again expecting a baby. They were delighted with their perfect eight pound, Alvin C., Jr.

When writing a book it is tempting for an author to do a little name dropping by choosing famous people of the present and past as examples showing the possibilities of going from rags to riches or from poverty to power — but in reality, these people are of little direct importance to you. This book has not been written for the rich, the powerful, the famous. It has been written especially for you. This book has been written so that you, your family, and friends can enjoy a great and abundant life.

BECOME A PSYCHIC ATHLETE

Maybe you began life from humble origin. "I started too far behind to ever catch up," you might say. Nothing is further from the truth. Cosmonomics has trained you to become a psychic athlete. I mean it very seriously when I say, "No matter how far behind you started in this race through life, you can be the winner!" And never let that thought drift far from your mind — you are the winner! You are the champion! It is you that can accomplish health, wealth, and happiness. If you settle for second place, you'll be second place. I want you to get the blue ribbon for winning this race.

ADVANCED UNIVERSAL MIND SECRETS

The power of the chant is often skimmed over lightly in occult writings. Most often it is neglected because many chants are the most powerful when spoken with the timing and the sounds that one might find written upon a sheet of music. It is difficult to express a melody with words so that it can be comprehended by the reader. Admittedly it is difficult, but the problem is not insurmountable if you take a moment to recall the musical scale you were taught in elementary school.

Before I continue, take a moment to practice your musical scale:

Do - re - me - fa - so - la - ti - do.

And then back down the scale:

Do - ti - la - so - fa - mi - re - do.

With your musical scale in mind, you are ready to advance to chants even more powerful than those previously revealed in these pages.

THE MYSTIC CHANT TO WIN
FRIENDS AND INFLUENCE PEOPLE

This powerful chant will teach you how to influence people and make them feel more friendly toward you. It is not just an everyday chant. It is a chant that should be reserved for those important moments in your life when your fate hinges upon the decisions of others.

HOW A COUNTY PLANNING
COMMISSION REVERSED ITS ACTION
AFTER FRED H. PERFORMED HIS MYSTIC CHANT

Fred H. purchased a valuable piece of real estate on the corner of a busy intersection in a northern California city. The property had been built originally as professional offices for doctors, dentists, and other medical related professions.

When Fred purchased the property, his intent was to use the building as offices for charitable and non-profit purposes.

When Fred and his attorney approached the County Planning Commission to change the zoning of his property from commercial to non-profit, his application was turned down (the county would be losing valuable taxes if the zoning were changed to "nonprofit").

Fred wasn't about to give up. He went right home and chanted like he had never chanted before.

It was difficult, but Fred persuaded his attorney to protest the ruling of the Planning Commission and ask that the application be reconsidered at the next Planning Commission meeting.

Fred was tense as the roll call voting began on his resubmitted application. The roll call stood at three Commissioners "for" and three "against," with one Commissioner still to vote.

Fred stared at the seventh Commissioner and with all the power at his command, concentrated on the thought that the still to vote Commissioner "do what he knows in his heart is right." The Commissioner voted "aye." Fred had won his appeal.

Fred told me later that the County Planning Commission had not overturned a single one of its own decisions during the past ten years.

Fred's attorney was flabbergasted after the hearing. "I just can't believe it," he said.

HOW TO PERFORM THE
MYSTIC CHANT THAT WILL
INFLUENCE OTHERS

The first thing to determine is that you have a just cause for concern, or that you might be treated unjustly when others are about to make decisions concerning your future, the future of a friend, or a family member.

First, familiarize yourself with the chant, and then I will teach you to chant the powerful words to simple notes upon the musical scale.

It is vitally important that you follow my instructions completely. Each note upon the musical scale sets up its own particular vibration which acts as a magnet that will draw the required power needed to the right place and at the right time.

> Any person in a position to direct my fate is now filled with a sense of justice and a desire to do that which is right.
>
> I hold no fear that any decision will be made that is not for my benefit or for my uplifting.
>
> The Ultra-Cosmonomic Power protects me from any force that is not of good.
>
> And so it is!

Now, practice your musical scale for a moment. This powerful chant only requires that you use the first three notes of the musical scale. Hum "do, re, mi; do, re mi," and then, "mi, re, do; mi, re, do." When this has been completed hum the musical notes up and down the scale: Do, re, mi; mi, re, do.

You're now ready to put your mystic chant into action. The chant should be sung with conviction. I have written the mystic chant again, showing which note should be sung with each word.

It is very simple to do. Just remember that you are merely going up and down the first three notes of the musical scale.

    do do re re mi mi re re do
    An-y per- son in a po- si- tion

    do re re   mi mi   re re
    to di- rect my fate is now

    do do re   re mi   mi re re
    fill- ed with a sense of jus-tice

    do do re re   mi mi re
    and a de- sire to do that

    re   do do   re re
    which is right. I hold

    mi mi   re   re do do re re
    no fear that an- y de- cis- ion

    mi   mi re   re   do do
    will be made that is not

    re   re   mi mi re re do
    for my ben- e- fit or for

    do   re   re   mi mi
    my up- lift- ing. The

    re   re do   do   re   re mi   mi
    Ul- tra- Cos- mo- nom- ic Pow- er

    re   re   do do   re   re mi
    pro- tects me from any for- ce

    mi   re re   do do
    that is not of good.

    re   re mi re
    And so it is!

I believe that you will be quite amazed at the miraculous power that this particular chant generates. It is not unusual to hear that the person performing this chant feels faint at its conclusion. Don't be alarmed if you experience similar sensations. Just sit down and relax for a few moments. The feeling of faintness will pass quickly.

HOW TO CHANT
LOVE INTO YOUR LIFE

It's very natural to want an abundance of love in your life. Aside from the physical pleasures of love, love gives one a sense of security, a sense of belonging, and a sense of worth. Indeed, there would be little satisfaction experienced from life if one did not have the feeling of not only loving, but of being loved as well.

No occult book would be complete without very explicit instructions on how one might attract an abundance of love into life. The love chant that will soon be revealed has worked wonders for others, as it will for you.

Love means many things to many people, and there are different types of love. Love of parent and children, husband and wife are but two examples of love. Because there are different kinds of love, it is essential that you face a particular direction when you perform your chant.

1. If you are desiring physical love, face north.
2. If you are seeking love of parent or children, face south.
3. If you are seeking more love from your mate or seeking the perfect mate, face toward the west.
4. If it is love of friends, colleagues, and acquaintances that you are desiring, turn toward the east.

If you are seeking more than one type of love, the chant must be repeated as you face each new direction.

THE CHANT OF THE NORTH

If it is physical love that you desire face toward the north and sing this powerful chant. It must be chanted slowly and in a monotone voice. The only musical note you will use from your musical scale is "do," the first note of your scale.

I am physically attractive. I radiate this beauty to all who cross my path of life. The beauty of my inner-self magnetically attracts my love to me. And so it is!

HOW ELAINE F. BECAME
BELLE OF THE BALL

Elaine F. was an ordinary looking woman of thirty-five. "If anyone wants to discuss my love-life," she said, "they can forget it. I don't have one!"

Elaine changed her attitude after performing her love chant of the north.

"It was time for the annual Christmas Ball, and as usual I didn't have a date. During past years I had simply stayed at home and sat around watching television and feeling sorry for myself. But this year I was determined that things would be different."

Elaine went on to say that she performed her love chant and had a sudden and "uncontrollable desire to buy a new ball gown, visit the beauty parlor, and do everything I could to make myself as attractive as possible."

Elaine didn't have a date for the Christmas Ball but she went anyway.

"I felt embarrassed walking into the Grand Ballroom unescorted, but the uncomfortable feeling I had soon left me. I was really the belle of the ball. I didn't miss one dance. I had the best time of my life, and I have to admit that I enjoyed the jealous looks of the other women at the ball.

"Did I find a husband? No! I wasn't looking for a husband. I was looking for love. I wouldn't trade the life I'm leading for a dozen husbands."

LOVE CHANT OF THE SOUTH

This chant is designed to bring closer cooperation and affection between the parent and child or the child to the parent.

This chant must be sung as you face the south. The two musical notes that you will be using are *re* and *mi*. To find the proper note on which to begin singing your musical scale: *do, re, mi, fa, so, la, ti, do*! Sing it again, paying particular attention to *re* and *mi*. If you for some reason find this *re* and *mi* chant difficult, chant it in a monotone voice, as you should any other chant that gives you difficulty as you progress through this chapter.

re   mi re mi   re mi   re
Gen- u- ine love, re- spect and

mi re mi   re mi   re mi re
a- ffec- tion is made man- i- fest

mi re mi re mi   re   mi   re
in my re- la- tion- ship with (*name*).

mi re   mi   re mi   re   mi re
All con- flict is now for- got- ten

mi re mi re   mi   re   mi
as we be- gin our new life

re mi   re   mi   re   mi   re mi re mi re mi
of love and Cos- mo- nom- ic co- op er- a- tion.

LOVE CHANT OF THE WEST

If you're seeking more love from your mate or are trying to find the perfect mate, then this chant is exactly what can make your desires become realities.

This chant uses your entire musical scale. It is not complicated. Simply begin at the bottom *do*, sing up your scale and then back down to your beginning note.

do   re   mi   fa   so la
The per- fect mate is in

ti   do ti la   so   fa
my li- fe. He/she will be

mi re   do re   mi fa
all good thi- ngs to me

so   la ti do   ti
and I to him/her. I

la   so   fa   mi   re
give more love than I

do do   do do   do do do do
re- ceive. My hap- pin- ess a- bounds.

HOW NORMAN N. USED THE LOVE CHANT
OF THE WEST TO WIN THE PERFECT MATE

Everyone believed that Norman N. was a confirmed bachelor — after all, he was forty and had never been married.

Norman wasn't a confirmed bachelor at all. He had just not been able to find the "woman of his dreams."

"There were many times," he said, "that I thought I had found the perfect woman, but something always happened to ruin our relationship before I could pop the question. I know that I was very set in my ways and that I had a very strong feeling as to what a marriage should really be."

Norman performed the love chant of the west, and within days he had found the "perfect" women and was madly in love.

Norman wrote later, "Quiet honestly, I didn't think the love chant would work, but something did! I had tried to find the perfect woman for years and had failed. Within days of chanting for the perfect mate Eunice came into my life. I just can't believe that it was a coincidence. I'd recommend the chant to anyone who was seriously interested in finding the perfect mate."

LOVE CHANT OF THE EAST

How to win the love and admiration of friends and colleagues no longer need be a problem. After you have performed the love chant of the east you'll never be on the "outside" again. More and more people will come to respect your opinion and your friendship. To put it simply, you will soon develop that indescribable magnetic personality.

Face toward the east, and sing your musical scale from the bottom. The notes you will sing are *fa, so, la, ti, do.* Pay particular attention to those sounds as you practice your scale. When ready, begin your chant.

fa so la ti   do do
I am a friend to all,

ti   la so fa fa   so
and all are a friend to

la ti do   do ti la so
me. The warmth and sin- cer- ity

fa fa so   la ti   do do ti   la so fa
of my new and pleas- ing per- son- al- i- ty

fa   so la ti do   do ti la
draws the best of friends to me now.

It may take a few moments to practice your musical scale before performing the love chants, but they are simple, and they do work. In performing the chants, you'll find your time well spent.

Years ago, a student asked if there wasn't a "miscellaneous" chant that he could use. "I don't want anything new added to my life," he said. "I just want a chant that will help me keep what I already have."

His request was a good one. Here is a general purpose chant that you can use to keep your life in balance and flood it with harmony.

THE GENERAL PURPOSE CHANT

This general purpose chant is a "shot in the arm," a spring tonic. It peps up your life to keep you healthy, happy, and whole.

This chant is written in eight lines. The entire first line is chanted to *do*. The entire second line to *re,* the third to *mi,* continuing upward through the scale.

This truly is a powerful chant. It fills you with love and self-confidence. When you have finished the chant you intuitively know that your future is filled with Cosmonomic sunshine.

During this chant, it makes no difference as to which direction you face. Most people report that they have felt the greatest power when they have sat in a chair facing the east. Use your intuition to discover the direction that best suits your own Cosmonomic personality.

do — I have no right to be poor.

re — I have no right to be lonely.

mi — I have no right to be ill.

fa — I have no right to be despondent.

so — I have no right to be friendless.

la — I *have* the right to be prosperous.

ti — I *have* the right to be happy, healthy and whole.

do — I *have* the right to claim all good, and I do!

THOUGH THE ORIGIN OF LUCKY CHARMS IS LOST IN ANTIQUITY THEIR POWER REMAINS

The rabbit's foot, the horsehoe, and the number 7. Millions of people look upon these objects as "lucky" charms. And to many of these people they probably are — mostly because they believe them to be lucky.

Men and women have acquired various objects to use as lucky charms since the dawn of civilization. When they did so and why they chose one object as being luckier than another remains lost in antiquity.

The origin of the belief in lucky charms is really an intellectual exercise for the scholar. The occultist knows that a lucky charm does have power. An acceptance of the principle that at sometime in history a superior intelligence, a cosmic mind revealed to man that material objects could be used as divine magnets to protect him from evil and draw good to him is all the information a Universal Mind student requires before beginning an adventure into creating his own lucky charms and talismans.

WHY YOUR LUCKY CHARM OR TALISMAN GENERATES POWER

Everything within the universe emits its own particular vibration or electrical energy. If used properly, this power can be directed and used to create a miracle or to draw good luck.

Your magic token or lucky charm becomes first a Cosmonomic laser beam. It shoots its power into the universe. It searches throughout the heavens until it discovers positive Universal Mind vibrations of like kind. When these positive vibrations are discovered, they are shot back to your lucky charm where they are magnetically attached. These atomic masses from the cosmos cling to your magic token and draw only good to you.

Many people who have never heard of Cosmonomics possess lucky charms that do work They work because they believe they will work. This blind belief in the power of a lucky charm creates its own power. The person owning such lucky charms has subconsciously performed many rituals to give their magic tokens mystic power.

Blind belief is a difficult mental state to acquire, and it is even more difficult to hold that belief for any lengthy period of time. It is for that reason that I will reveal a ritual that you can consciously perform to create your own lucky charm — and it makes little difference that others believe in its power or not. It still works wonders!

LUCINDA V. MADE HER OWN LUCKY CHARM AND WON THE MAN SHE LOVED

Lucinda V. was an ordinary young woman in her late twenties. She had been in no hurry to marry, but as thirty began to approach she became apprehensive that she might grow old without ever finding the man she could love enough to marry.

Lucinda was a popular young woman. She never lacked for dates or men in her life, but she just did not want any of them as her husband.

"I honestly believed that lucky charms were a bunch of hocus-pocus," Lucinda said, "until a girl friend of mine created what she called a 'magic token.' So many good things began happening to her after she began carrying her lucky charm that I had to admit that the unbelievable string of good luck had to be more than coincidence."

Lucinda inquired of her girl friend as to how she might make a lucky token for herself.

"I still wasn't convinced when I began the ritual to create a magic token that any lucky charm would find the man for me, but I was willing to give it a try. But before I had completed the ritual, a strange feeling overcame me. I suddenly knew that my lucky charm really was magic and that it would work, and it did!"

After Lucinda created her lucky charm, she was invited to attend a dance that was given by the local chapter of a single parents organization.

"I really didn't want to go to the dance," she said, "but deep inside I intuitively knew that I should go.

"On the way to the dance I kept thinking, 'why in the world am I going to a dance that's for divorced or widowed parents?' Within minutes of arriving at the dance I had my answer. Tony came to our table and asked me to dance. It was love at first sight.

"When Tony asked me to the beach the next day with him and his two children, I was apprehensive. I wasn't sure that I was ready to accept a ready-made family, and how would the children react to me?

"I need not have worried about the children. Within minutes of our first meeting we hit it off perfectly.

"Tony and I were married, and I have never been happier. The children call me 'mother,' and I couldn't love them more.

"I suppose it could all just be a coincidence, but it seems strange that I had spent years looking for the perfect man without success, but within days of creating my own lucky charm I had found the perfect mate."

THE UNIVERSAL RITUAL
THAT WILL CREATE A LUCKY CHARM

Anything can become your lucky charm, but for practical purposes it is wise to chose an object that is small enough to carry or to wear upon your person. A coin, ring, or any other such object is appropriate. One student carried a simple paper clip in his pocket as a magic token and had spectacular results from his efforts.

Before beginning your ritual, wash the object that you have chosen as your lucky charm in very warm, but not hot water. If the

object that will soon become magical has been handled by many
people (such as a coin), add a pinch of salt to the warm water. Salt
has a purifying effect and has very important uses in occultism. It
drives away negative thoughts, bad luck, evil spirits, and the like.

When your token has been cleansed lay it on the table and sit
yourself comfortably before it. You are now going to use a double
word pyramid to create your very own unique lucky charm.

Hold your hands approximately six inches above your token.
Imagine within your mind that waterfalls of energy are cascading
from your hands onto the charm. When you feel the energy
flowing from your hands repeat these magical words aloud.

I
whis - per
these words u-
pon the winds of
the Cos - mo - nom - ic
cur - rent of good for - tune

My lu - cky ch - arm is now
draw - ing ev - ery good thing
to me now and for -
ever more. My ev -
ery wish is
now ful -
filled.

HOW TO USE GEMS TO BRING LOVE, HAPPINESS, AND PROSPERITY INTO YOUR LIFE

In Psychic Telemetry I revealed the power of the gem when
used as a healing tool, but gems are much more than Cosmonomic
medicine. Gems can be used to miraculously attract into your life
every one of your desires.

When I use the word gem I do not necessarily refer to
precious gems. I refer to a gem as any stone that has proven occult
significance, though many of these can be precious gems. All of
the stones that you might require for Cosmonomic purposes can
be purchased at your local rock shop at a very modest cost.

THE BLUE GEMS ARE YOUR
SPIRITUAL GEMS

Stones that are of the bluish tints are the stones that will draw spiritual unfolding, cleanse the conscience, and uplift the spirit. These gems should be worn or carried whenever you wish to draw spiritual values into your life.

Lavender and purple are considered blue tones, but they are exceptions to the general occult rules.

Gems of the lavender and purple tones are worn to protect you from curses, evil thought forces, and other destructive agencies. They should also be worn if you are trying to capture someone within your own thought force.

HOW ALFRED L. USED A POWERFUL GEM
TO BREAK A LIFE-LONG CURSE

Alfred L. was living in a cosmopolitan city on the West Coast. Alfred was a very cultured individual, a man that no one would guess was born and reared in the back woods of the Appalachian Mountains. Even less would one suspect that Al, the "man who had everything," was threatened by a life-long curse that stretched back through his family for four generations.

According to Alfred, his great-great grandfather had jilted a young girl who was carrying his child. The girl's family was outraged and pronounced a curse upon the wayward suitor and "the first born son of every generation forevermore."

Al's great-great grandfather became insane as had the first-born son of the generation which followed. Al was one of these first-born sons and lived in constant fear that he too would go mad at any moment. Al wrote to a friend about the curse.

> I had heard that the amethyst was a stone that should be worn by any person persecuted by an unjust curse. I lived in constant fear that the curse would manifest itself at any time.
>
> I was desperate as I bought an amethyst ring and slipped it on my finger. I can't explain in words what the feeling that overwhelmed me was really like. Peace? Confidence? I don't

know the words to describe the wonderful feeling within. I do know that the curse was broken and that I was at last safe.

All of my friends envied me as the man who had everything. Little did they know the constant fear under which I lived. Now when people say "I envy you," I answer "You're right! I do have everything."

THE RED GEMS ARE YOUR
PHYSICAL STONES

Any gems with definite tones of red can be used to attract physical love, vigor, vitality, youth, and better physical health.

The red stones are powerful and should not be misused. Remember that these stones are physical magnets. They do not govern the higher emotions or more positive thoughts.

HOW TO GAIN EMOTIONAL
SECURITY BY WEARING GREEN STONES

The green gems attract the highest of emotional feelings. Love, children, tolerance, general healing, calmness of the spirit, and love of the home are all governed by the powerful stones with the hue of green.

YELLOW GEMS GOVERN
THE INTELLECT

Gems that are yellow in nature govern things of the mind. If you are studious, need to make plans, memorize complex details, or improve your reading skills, then yellow is the color for you.

THE DIAMOND WILL
ATTRACT PROSPERITY

Diamonds have always been thought of as symbols of wealth, and they are. A certain amount of wealth is needed to purchase diamonds. One can easily see why diamonds are evidence of a person's wealth, but to the student of Universal Mind, diamonds are not only evidence of wealth, they attract wealth.

If you want to attract certain wealth, make the diamond your magic token.

THE GEMSTONE POWER AFFIRMATION

To give your gem or stone added power so that it might quickly bring to you your heart's desire, I will reveal a powerful occult affirmation.

First, place your stones upon the table and hold your hands in the same manner as creating a lucky charm. When all is ready, repeat this affirmation three times:

> The Universal Mind of the great creative universe now hears my declaration and bends to my command. I now command that his stone attract (your desire) to me at the proper time and by the proper method. And so it is!

THERE CAN BE NO EXCUSE
FOR CLINGING TO AN UNHAPPY LIFE

If you cling to an unhappy life it is because you want to. It is not because you have to. Universal Mind has given you the opportunity to become one with the creative force of the entire universe. The simple satisfaction of this personal communion would be worth any effort, but it is only half of the entire whole.

First you experienced the communion, but that is not enough. You must follow up this cosmic communion by expressing all of the positive rewards of this cosmic immersion — health, happiness, prosperity, and love. Do not settle for half the loaf. Demand the entire loaf and it will be yours.

LET YOUR NEW UNIVERSAL MIND
POWER BRING ECSTASY, PLENTITUDE,
AND ABUNDANT HEALTH

In this book I have not taught you intangible philosophical principles. I have taught you how to achieve concrete results in the pursuit of any desire. I have taught you to knock away the obstacles that may hinder your journey toward completely harmonious living — and I have taught you how to keep those obstacles from returning.

There is nothing that can stop you now. No one can beat you at the race of life as long as you keep your Cosmonomic motor running. Money, health, love, and happiness will be yours forevermore.

Now step out into a world filled with rainbows — each rainbow with its own particular pot of gold waiting quietly and just for *you*!

And so it is!